Testimonials

What's All This?

This collection calls to mind a retrospective of an artist's life work. The time span and breadth of material covered will speak with immediacy to the needs of many different readers: people struggling to find meaning in the challenges of life; women yearning for the inner authority of the authentic self in a patriarchal society; men seeking powerful and inclusive images of masculinity that give honour to sacred sexuality; people who have been through dark times in the belly of the whale; and those who wonder about the mystery of dreams, to name just a few.

Victoria Castiglione

A unifying principle throughout these wide-ranging essays is the assertion that aspects of Jung's work can be used as spiritual practices that integrate well with the Christian story. The essays take the reader to deep places of reflection through an easy conversational style.

Gary Commins DD

The Treasures of Darkness

Darkness is often understood as that which is to be feared, whether as the "Shadow" in our inner lives or when experienced culturally as racism or evil. In this essay, we are invited to explore our positive experiences of darkness. We are encouraged to welcome and integrate the darkness, to strive for balance between light and dark, and to consider the possibility that there are blessings to be found in acknowledging the treasures of darkness.

Norma Dody

Empowerment from Within: Listening to the Soul

George puts into words an experience that is so real, so raw, so lived, that it is very difficult to get a perspective on. He is absolutely spot on, in my experience, in his coalescence of Germain Greer's ideas that there is a simple clarity of self that exists for the prepubescent girl. And that "affirming, protecting, and exploring the self-vision of childhood is an essential task for women in their search for sacred self-fulfilment."

Brittain Garrett

Spirituality and Psychotherapy

This exploration of spirituality and psychotherapy is thought provoking and insightful. It has led me to reflect more deeply on the relationship between these concepts in my own practice. George's approach is one of inclusivity and the reflections are offered through his self-proclaimed circumambulating style.

Antonia R Clissa

My Experience of Self

George has created a refreshing and easy-to-read reflection on the individuation process and how it relates to the Christ Story. His ability to speak his own truth gently encourages us to continue to engage with our own individuation process and to live it out in our shared lives.

Maree White

Masculine Spirituality

Affirming the separation of masculinity and patriarchy, celebrating the variety of expressions of the masculine, and stressing the integration of the feminine for male development, all this resonated deeply with me. My favourite part of this essay was the emphasis on 'embodied cognition.' It is incredibly important to my own understanding of the masculine energy and represents a crucial path forward in my own development.

Matt Lord

The Jonah Syndrome: Do You Get It?

"The Jonah story was little more than a quirky story in my spiritual life before George's reflections. Now, I feel as though I see it with entirely fresh eyes. It has helped me view times spent stuck in the 'belly' in an entirely new light. The questions of how we listen and, perhaps more commonly, do not listen to the voice of divinity seems central to most of life's difficulties. In that spirit, this exploration of Jonah's story has encouraged me to summon the courage to listen more deeply to where I am actually being led, even when it is not always a place I would initially like to go!"

Dominic Fay

The Initiated Male: What About me?

A timely read. I read this essay as I was navigating the difficult terrain of the unexpected and unwanted end of my ten-year relationship. George's exploration of male initiation has helped me reframe the sometimes-senseless pain of the end of my love, the death of my hopes, and the loss of my home. The initiation experience he describes invites me to discover myself moving into an uncharted adventure that has meaning and vibrant possibilities. He captures the sense of new life that is emerging for me as I let go of old ways of self-understanding and am initiated into a surprising future.

Ashley Brown

The Initiated Male: What about Me? invites readers to consider how life beckons each one of us to live more wholly through the experience of 'initiation'. George proves a trustworthy companion throughout this reflective orientation. Accessible, erudite, and compelling, readers will be well-positioned to attune to the signposts of initiation, and perhaps most importantly, better enabled to choose 'the enlarged life' in light of this awareness.

Lachlan Savill

Stepping Into the Christ Myth

This reflection has caused me to examine my own relation to Christ. It reinforces for me that the Incarnation is an ongoing phenomenon, a celebration of the Divine living and present in all of us, the Christ in all things. I hope that, in revisiting the heart of this reflection, I will be able to escape my own constrictions that have made Christ too narrow and too limited.

Mary Martin Stump

What If? Reconsidering my Shadow

This essay is that rarest of species, an original contribution to an over-populated field. It is original in both theory and practice and deserves wide circulation.

Sally Kester PhD

I find it interesting and refreshing to consider the Shadow as non-adversarial, as a partner, a helper, companion, and not an enemy. It brings her into the village. If the Shadow is to be helper and partner, I need to see her as a mirror image of me. The questions I am left with from George's reflection are: What does a partnership/helper model of my Shadow mean for me in my psyche and in my body? Is it possible?

Gabrielle Dean

About the Author

Throughout the course of his youth and adult life George has been focused on the interface between the psychology of Carl Jung and Christian Spirituality. This has been expressed in priestly ministry and spiritual direction, and currently in psychotherapy, counseling, peace and nonviolence education and artwork.

George is committed to promoting Jung's psychological insights as contemporary spiritual practice for the wellbeing of individuals and for the Common Good. He lives in Western Australia.

georgetrippe@gmail.com

Also by George E. Trippe

Nonviolent Spirituality:
A Personal Reflection

There were a few moments when I literally gasped. Readers are in for a treat. *Ann Morgan, PhD*

As a white practitioner of racial reconciliation in South Africa I find George's embodied, accessible exploration of Nonviolent Spirituality very useful indeed.
Wilhelm Verwoerd, PhD

How Did I Get Here?
Reflecting on my Principles for Nonviolent Living

A truly insightful piece of writing that has significantly changed my approach to the way I live my life.
Adrian Pizzata

What an incredible privilege. I am certain I will return to this work at many points throughout my life.
Timothy McInnes

Who Said That?
The Spirited Practice of Active Imagination

Such clarity in writing and teaching! *Pauline Kennedy*

What's All This?

Essays Supporting Enspirited Lives

George E. Trippe, PhD

First published 2023 by George E. Trippe, PhD

Produced by Independent Ink
independentink.com.au

Copyright © George Trippe 2023

The moral right of the author to be identified as the author of this work has been asserted.

All rights reserved. Except as permitted under the Australian Copyright Act 1968, no part of this publication may be reproduced, stored in a retrieval system, or transmitted in any form or by any means, electronic, mechanical, photocopying, recording or otherwise, without prior written permission from the publisher. All enquiries should be made to the author.

Cover design by Independent Ink
Internal design by Independent Ink
Edited by Victoria Castiglione
Typeset in 12.5/17 pt Adobe Garamond Pro by Post Pre-press Group, Brisbane
Cover image: by the author

ISBN 978-0-6454243-6-2 (paperback)
ISBN 978-0-6454243-7-9 (epub)

Disclaimer:
Any information in the book is purely the opinion of the author based on personal experience and should not be taken as business or legal advice. All material is provided for educational purposes only. We recommend to always seek the advice of a qualified professional before making any decision regarding personal and business needs.

Contents

Introduction 1

The Wounded Healer 5
The Treasures of Darkness 19
Empowerment from Within: Listening to the Soul 41
Spirituality and Psychotherapy 57
My Experience of Self 83
Masculine Spirituality 89
The Jonah Syndrome: Do You Get It? 99
The Initiated Male: What About Me? 135
Images of Transformation 155
Creating Inclusive Organisations 175
Stepping Into the Christ Myth 183
What If? Reconsidering My Shadow 193

Afterword 211
Acknowledgements 215

Introduction

Here's the picture: a parent walks into a room and there are items spread all around the place, on the floor and the furniture. Standing with hands on hips the parent asks, "What's all this?" It is up to the reader to decide whether the parent is angry, frustrated, amused, bewildered, all of the above, none of these.

Several months ago, in a conversation with my colleague, Wilhelm Verwoerd, in South Africa, we talked about the need to engage and explore more fully the experience of darkness. I mentioned that I thought I had some notes on the treasures of darkness that I had filed away and had not ever used. He was interested so I went looking and found more than I had remembered. Those notes are now reformatted in a reflection in this collection. This exercise led me to realise that I have a significant number of outline notes and full texts for oral presentations from over thirty years tucked away in computer files. I went hunting and this present collection is the result of my search. As I surfed my computer files thinking about this notion of a collection of essays, the image of the cluttered room and the parent asking the title question came to mind: *What's all this?* The parent in me stands shaking his head and chuckling. He is quite amazed at the work that these files represent. It has been a privilege over these years to have been offered many different opportunities in which to speak about matters of the soul that are important to me.

My review of these files has affirmed again that I have had, and still have, a deep desire to integrate my understanding of the psychology of Carl Jung with the spiritual frame that is central to my life. This desire grew out of my lived experience as a youth in an unusual parish community. Both priests were deeply committed to Jung's work. One was my first therapist, the other my first spiritual director. Through them I undertook psycho-spiritual reflective and devotional practices based on Jung's work largely through journal writing and the experience of working with my dreams. While many aspects of my life have changed over the years, these practices and this desire have remained constant. I am more than ever convinced that aspects of Jung's psychological work can be used as spiritual practices that integrate well with the Christian story and other religious containers. This is particularly true of dream work and active imagination. The dialogue with, and the integration of, Jung's work with Christian spirituality continues to engage my energy and interest. I have chosen this collection because they represent my efforts in very different forums to offer insight into this integrative work.

Though I have composed several of these essays in written form, most were shared originally as oral presentations. In reformatting them I have edited them as seems appropriate, and some more than others. It is inevitable that some themes and stories are repeated in different places. It is also inevitable that my ideas over time have changed, and I may seem to contradict myself. The older I become the more I see change as a sign of continued

Introduction

and deeper insight in the mysteries of life. The older I get the more I am suspicious of well-ordered and consistent thinking; complexity and confusion, even mystery make more sense. These essays are each stand-alone works from a particular time and occasion. They need not be read in order. I have placed them in order based on the date I created the original notes or outline. These essays-reflections represent my having lived many years in a sacred space combining Jung's work and a more liberal Christian spiritual frame. I am content still to live here.

I hope readers will engage and be intrigued, provoked, and edified. Many years ago, a wise woman once commented to me that my task in my chosen work was to ask questions, not to have answers. I hope that these reflections raise more questions than answers. If so, I am very satisfied.

George E. Trippe, PhD
February 2023

The Wounded Healer

The first presentation of this reflection was in 1988 in Western Australia. I later presented the reflections at a weekend conference at Epiphany Church, Odenton, Maryland, USA, in March 1992. I have worked here from the early outline notes to create a fresh reflection on this ancient and sacred image. I begin with a story I have told elsewhere that is pivotal to my life.

Stories

It was 28 March 1973. After years of ignoring my discomfort, I faced the fact squarely that I have an addictive personality; I was, I am an alcoholic. After having delivered the kids to pre-school, it was a tearful drive home and yet a more tearful conversation-confession with my wife Shirley. She had been worried and was glad I had come to this realisation. I soon got in touch with a good friend who was in AA and told him my story. We then met daily over the next week or so. He was incredibly helpful and encouraging. There was no judgement, a wee bit of practical advice and companionship. AA meetings were not possible at that time, so he became my AA meeting. Another friend from AA also joined us as support. The two of them provided what I needed to stay with the decision I wanted now so badly to keep.

My mother shared an encounter with me at an important time in her life. She underwent a radical mastectomy many years ago, and while still in hospital a woman came to visit her in her room. The woman shared her experience of having had a mastectomy and gave my mother very helpful insights and practical information as to the recovery experience. My mother was greatly helped by this stranger who shared her similar journey.

Why do I tell these stories? As I begin to explore the ancient image of the wounded healer, why start here? The supportive actions of my friend and this stranger demonstrate the role of the wounded healer. Out of their own past wounds and struggles, his with addiction and hers with a serious surgery, they offered support, counsel, and encouragement. In my mother's case the woman came, gave her gift of shared experience, and went on her way. In my case, my friend and I remained in touch over many years right up until his death a few years ago. The gift he gave me was to believe in me until I had the confidence to believe in myself. At a time when I was very fragile and uncertain, he was a lifesaver for me.

The Image

The Wounded Healer is a sacred and powerful image in many religious traditions, including the Christian. Among many cultures including those in Africa, Asia, Siberia and North America, the

Shaman carries the wounded healer role. In many instances the qualification for the Shaman was a wounding experience in a dream or vision. In some cultures, dreams of dismemberment were dramatic and signalled a call and initiation into the role. It was considered essential for the Shaman to have been struck down, wounded in some way, in order to serve the people as an interpreter and mediator of the world of the gods. This is the common core of the archetypal wounded healer role.

In the Christian faith tradition, it is Jesus as the Christ who carries the wounded healer image and role in the community. In Christ's story, the image of the wounded healer begins to take shape in the temptations in the desert and comes to fruition in the death and resurrection events. The imagery in the Biblical book of Isaiah, chapter 53, helps give shape and understanding to the role that Jesus lived out. The Isaiah passage is a common reading on Good Friday in many Christian churches. The traditional theology of the saving work of the Christ draws on these images from Isaiah, specifically in reference to the crucifixion. "This servant ... bore ... the stripes by which we are healed" (Isa. 53:5). In the Biblical Gospel texts, we read that Jesus lived out the wounded healer role in a variety of experiences of suffering, including in the fasting and temptations in the desert, in his weeping over Jerusalem, in prayerful agony in the garden of Gethsemane and finally in his death on the cross. These are his wounds that heal the faithful.

The primary focus of the suffering Christ is the crucifixion. It is the culmination, or the summary, of all his sufferings. The faith tradition affirms that the sufferings of Jesus are voluntary acts of love in which he confronts evil, death, and sin, and the depth of his love shatters their deathly grip. Such is the power of love, of voluntary sacrifice, of wounds endured in love. The tradition teaches that the sufferings of Jesus are acts of love that declare an ultimate victory over the powers of evil in the world.

Implications

There are three implications here that are important for us. First, there is a link made between voluntary, intentional suffering and love. The energy of love is intimately woven into the tapestry of this interpretation. It is the love of Jesus for the people that motivates his actions that lead to and include his death. As we explore the wounded healer image in the context of the Jesus story, we can affirm the link between voluntary, intentional suffering and love. It is core to the Jesus story and instructive for us in terms of the healing nature of suffering love.

Second, again in the context of this story, it is possible to confirm the truth that suffering need not be meaningless. Regardless of how the event or events of suffering have come about, there is possible insight, meaning and benefit tucked away in the circumstances of the event. This is critical for us. It is possible to wrestle from our sufferings deep and lasting values that assists us living more complete lives. As a youth my mentor once said to me, "Suffering equals maturity." I like this no more now than I did then, but here sits solidly a troubling truth. Even my sufferings and wounds come to me carrying the possibility of meaning for my wholeness.

Third, after the pattern of Christ our wounds can be a possible blessing for others. The friend who walked with me in the choice for sobriety, and the stranger who assisted and encouraged my mother demonstrate this. Here we come to our personal experiences of the wounded healer and to the challenges and tasks that this archetypal image asks of us. I am summoned to do my inner work, in order to enable the healing of others.

The Work

How do we do this inner work? It seems to me that in Jesus we see a man who knew himself deeply and accepted the challenges of his life and the tasks involved. He understood and accepted who he was and what he was summoned to do. For me the pattern transfers when I understand and accept who I am as fully as I am able, and embrace the wounds that come to me in life. I suggest that it is the ego conscious me, "I," who takes the role of the suffering one under the tutelage of the Christ within. It is the ego who suffers the pain and humiliation of the wound however it has come, from within or from outside. "I" choose voluntarily, as an act of self-love to engage the wounds, inner or outer. "I" choose to be crucified between the opposing, sometimes many and varied responses to the wounding experience, and to work step by step toward resolution. I am informed and guided by both the Christ of the tradition in Jesus and the Christ within my own soul. It is from this inner transformative work under the guidance of the Christ image and energy, that I come to deeper experiences of self-understanding and self-love. From this soul work can emerge a new pathway, a new direction, and a new sense of who I am. Out of the healing of my wounds over time, whatever their origin, I am then able to offer this same compassion and love to others that I have given to myself as guided by the Christ. The work of the wounded healer begins here with my inner work.

For me this work has come to include reframing the traditional substitutionary theory of Jesus' actions, and to withdraw my projections from him as the one who has done it all for all time. Christ in Jesus, for me is the one who shows the way. He embraced the destiny of his own life and lived it at a very high price. I am summoned to follow this way and to embrace my life in all its fullness regardless of the cost. The challenge is to be me and no other, as Christ was himself and no other.

Years ago in Los Angeles, at a conference introducing a training program for spiritual directors, a colleague posed a question in relation to this wounded healer image. He asked: "Are we wounded healers or wounded wounders?" He went on later to state that the story of the temptations of Jesus reminds us that even for Jesus there are no shortcuts. He did his work; we must do ours. If we do not, it is possible we will pass on our unresolved hurts, angers, fears, and pains, and spread the misery, rather than share the harvest of the wounds we have come to accept, and the amazing surprises and benefits they give us. The woman who visited my mother had done her work and shared from her deep acceptance. My friend from AA was doing his work, and I received the supportive benefits.

In the pattern of the Christ in Jesus, it is a remarkable and ongoing mystery that my brokenness may well be the most useful part of me for others. I have come to refer to this as "consecrated brokenness." My wounds and difficult experiences may be my most sacred resources for others. If I can embrace my wounds, my fragility, uncertainty, failures, limits, weaknesses, if I can love these in me, then I can stand with you on a level playing field, with no pretence of righteousness or superiority, and meet you with compassion and empathy. The wounded healer comes to any encounter from a place of deep self-acceptance, and offers compassion, companionship, a wee bit of advice perhaps and quiet acceptance, encouragement, and love.

The challenge of the archetype of the wounded healer is to do our own inner work. If we do not, we risk being those wounded wounders who share our misery. Our work, our spiritual practices give birth to the compassion and empathy in us that enables us to walk with others in their trials and offer life giving support and care.

Healing

There are several aspects of the healing experience to consider here as we reflect on our own healing and then on our ability to be wounded healers for others. First, our self-awareness and acceptance are essential if we are to experience any significant healing. If we remain unaware of, or deny, our own wounds, there is almost no chance that we can be healing agents for others; and acknowledging our wounds is not enough. We must do something with this awareness that will allow for healing. In raising the image of the wounded wounder, my colleague's concern was that through our lack of self-awareness, too often we wound others; we will cripple rather than heal, because we have not come to any appreciable awareness of our own wounds. I have come to understand that if I won't deal with my anger, I cannot help others to deal their anger. If I won't sort out my relationship to alcohol, how can I assist others who seek to do this? On several occasions I have had individuals tell me that they felt let down by people they consulted about their struggles with alcohol. Sometimes those consulted would try to minimize or dismiss the concern. If we are to be wounded healers, we must first become clear about the wounds we carry in our own souls and continue to deal with them so that we are able to be helpful to others. In my understanding of spiritual practice, I affirm that the issues of self-awareness, self-knowledge, and self-understanding are critical to a mature and wholesome spiritual life. The sixteenth century Carmelite mystic, Teresa of Avila, saw this as the starting place, the place of entry in the spiritual quest. Healing begins with self-awareness.

Second, from this first point we remember that the experience of healing is most often a process; rarely is it an instantaneous event. This is particularly true of wounds in the soul. Healing takes time. Often the wound needs to be considered from various points of view and over time. In my own relationship with alcohol, stopping drinking was only the first step in the process. Over the next several years I had to learn a great deal about myself, to ground the healing process and to prevent a relapse into the bottle. I had to re-evaluate the way I handled stress, and particularly my anger; I had to learn about my general attitudes toward problem solving; I was confronted with the compulsive nature of my own personality, which made consuming alcohol such an attractive past time. I had to face that I was an addictive person in numerous ways, and that I would continue to bounce from addiction to addiction until I understood this about myself. While the healing process is at times accelerated, most of the time healing takes time. A friend of mine is fond of saying that it takes an entire lifetime to make a human being. Things take time, healing is its own process.

Several years ago, a man who sought my counsel had a dream which challenged him to consider how he got to the depths of depression, so that he could prevent this from happening again. He saw the challenge as enormous, like a task for the rest of his life. He had to learn, as we all must, that healing often involves every aspect of our lives, and is a life-long process. Healing takes time.

Another aspect of the nature of the healing process is that life seems to have ways of presenting us with the issues that need our attention, one after the other. It seems there is almost always a concern or problem to engage and with which to deal. Many years ago in a brief conversation, Morton Kelsey chuckled as he assured me that we could trust life to bring up the next item on life's agenda, we didn't need to go hunting for it.

Third, along with understanding healing as a process comes the challenge of knowing one's own limits. Paul, in the Biblical writings claimed that he could be all things to all people. Fine for him, but I cannot, and I have not seen this ability in any other person I know. For each of us there are limits; there are situations in which we do not function well, and where we cannot effectively enact the role of the wounded healer. I affirm that, for me, this is okay. My limits came home to me clearly once when I was asked to come to the home of an older man who had a problem with alcohol. I was not aware until I got there that he was drunk. It was the bottle talking in a long process of nonsensical chatter and lament. I found the process very painful, and I could do nothing; the situation touched on my own wounds. I left knowing that I did little for him. Never again. I am willing to work with anyone on the issue of substance abuse, but I do not handle well the person who is drunk. That is over my limit. It is important to understand that we each have situations in which we cannot function creatively for others.

Fourth, this brings us to the simple realisation that not everything in life gets fixed. There are some things that are healed only in the sense that we learn to carry our wounds with patience, humility, and a growing trust in ourselves to practice self-care. In reference to others, Anthony Storr, in his book, *Solitude*, asserts that this is not healing through insight, nor through solving specific problems, but through making a new and better relationship with the other, inner, or outer. It is healing by means of a change of attitude.

For me the healing of my attitude in reference to my back condition has been a life-changing experience. The condition I live with is from birth and began to cause me pain in my early twenties. Since then, pain is a frequent companion. I do well all things considered, largely through a change of attitude. I have moved beyond my original rage and anger and have been able to accept my limitations and come to see my back as a friend who travels with me and challenges me to practice responsible self-care. My back is not better as I age, but I am, and I do well in the larger picture of my life.

Too often we can develop an attitude toward life that expects that, as faithful people, it is only a matter of time before all our problems will be solved, all our pain and strife will ease, and all our wounds will be healed. These expectations have no basis in living reality. They set us up for all sorts of disappointment and disillusionment as life continues to unfold, and they risk being destructive to living a creative life within our limits.

As wounded healers, often those wounds that have been healed in some way still carry something of the old energy in them. While I have helped many people come to sobriety, I still have moments when I feel the quiet urge toward alcohol and in those moments endure a significant discomfort.

I have wondered at times if many of us carry what might be called a life wound, a wound that has a long-term impact on our character. Perhaps it is a childhood illness from which we have recovered, but that has shaped the way we see the world and live in it. It may be an ongoing, limiting condition that travels with us over many years as companion in our daily living. In terms of healing, the acceptance of these various conditions, events and influences can have a substantial impact on our character and often play a key role in humanising us in ways we cannot imagine or understand. Years ago, a Jungian Analyst commented to me that someday I might come to see my back condition as my greatest friend. It has taken me a very long time to understand her comment. I realise in these older years that this life-long condition, this life wound, has had a substantial influence on who I have been and am still becoming.

Healing requires self-awareness, healing is a process, healing involves limits, healing changes attitudes, and all these invite us to be clear about our understanding of healing and the notion of perfection. What is it to be healed, to be well? What is it to be perfect? Our use of the word perfect in everyday English is not remotely connected to the Greek word that we find in the well-known teaching attributed to Jesus in the Biblical book of Matthew. The English translation of Matthew 5:48 reads: "Be perfect therefore as your heavenly father is perfect." In our common usage today the word "perfect" means without mistake, blemish, spot of sin; flawless, 100%; it implies the exclusion of the flawed and blemished; it has no room for error or mistake. The Greek meaning of the term in Matthew 5:48 does not mean that at all. It means to be complete, rounded out; it has to do with totality, brought to the fullness of being, it implies the inclusion of all things. It also has an end purpose in mind, toward which it moves. To redefine perfection in the Biblical understanding invites us to realise that to be healed in the deepest sense means to include all that is and has been our life into a whole, single, simple offering to God. What is it then to be whole and complete?

The diagnosis of my back condition at age twenty-two invited me into this life-long reflection. Several years later the issue became real for me again when as a part of my education in pastoral care, I was assigned to call weekly on a woman in Philadelphia General Hospital. She had been in her ward for forty-seven years when I met her; the ward was her home. She was well except that she couldn't walk. Over those years she had worked in the hospital in various ways, and from her point of view she lived a full life within her limits. She remarked one day that pneumonia the year before had slowed her down a little, otherwise she was fine. I remember her with no small amount of awe. I sat there weekly wearing my back brace and sharing conversation with her and was challenged to reflect on healing and being well. She knew her limits; she was not perfect or "fixed." Her healing was of her attitude over time. She embraced her sadness and regret and lived as fully as she could within her own limited world. I experienced her as a remarkable woman who was far more well than I. What is it to be healed, to be well?

Some years later in California, I saw the almost disastrous effects of the simplistic confusion that can result when we do not reflect carefully on healing and perfection. I encountered a group of young adults who had become quite involved in enthusiastic renewal aspects of Christian spiritual practices. Among their number was a young woman who lived with cerebral palsy. Life had been difficult, and she was a battler and had done amazingly well. In their enthusiasm some of the group encouraged her to pray more fervently to be completely healed. The message came through clearly: "All you need is a little more faith, and you can throw away those crutches." It didn't happen and she ended up attempting suicide. She failed at that, thank God, and part of her recovery was to separate from that misguided group, and find a more life-giving spirituality and supportive community. She was not perfect, but experienced deep healing and was more complete. What is it to be healed?

Conclusion

The challenge of the wounded healer image invites us into a deeper understanding of healing. Engaging our own healing and enabling the healing of others requires substantial and disciplined self-awareness; it is most often a process that can unfold over many years; it involves embracing our limits and boundaries; it often involves us in a change of attitude toward our wounds, and summons us to include all of who we are and all that we experience into a whole life that is full, meaningful, purposeful and profoundly satisfying.

While the image of the wounded healer appears to be focused on looking out toward others and what we offer them, the experience of this archetype begins with each of us engaging ourselves. We prepare to undertake this archetypal, ancient role of compassion and empathy first by doing our own soul work. We begin by dealing with our wounds and letting the Christ energy within the depths of our souls support us in the process of our own healing. Having engaged ourselves we are then able, like the friend who walked with me, and the woman who came to my mother's bedside, to enact the remarkable mystery of the wounded healer in simple, ordinary, and life-giving ways.

The Treasures of Darkness

In a conversation with my colleague Wilhelm Verwoerd in South Africa, we focused briefly on the experience of darkness and the need to explore it. As I mention in the Introduction, I remembered that I had put some notes in a computer file under the title, Treasures of Darkness some time ago and I went looking for them. To my surprise they were dated 1990. While I have included more recent thoughts in this essay, I have worked largely from my original notes and place this according to the date of that original work.

Introduction

Following an ancient teaching practice, I begin by stringing some "beads" that together create a framework for reflection.

— A friend of some forty years once told me that in his 70s he still needed to have a light on when he went to bed to sleep.

He was not comfortable with the dark. Another young man in his twenties also told me that he was afraid of the dark, especially at night in bed.
- A man in his middle years shared with me that he was very aware of the darkness within him, but he just did not want to go there for fear of what he would find.
- Another young man once shared a dream in which he stood before a darkened room with the door slightly open. He knew he was meant to enter, but he was afraid and slowly stuck his arm and hand around to the other side of the door to see if he could find out what might be there. He did not go into the dark room.
- Many years ago, when our children were quite young, we visited a deep cave at a tourist location in Arizona. A guide took us by elevator deep down into the cave, and after his talk he switched off the lights for a short moment so that we could experience total darkness. I was a bit shaken and two of my children were holding very tightly to my pant legs.
- A friend once told me of a friend of his who jokingly showed him a pure white canvas and declared that it was a painting of a polar bear in a snowstorm.
- In an interview relating to dreams, a therapist remarked that Christians suffer from too much light.
- As boys we were told never to look directly into the sun as that intense light would damage our eyes and blind us.

This string of beads forms a backdrop as we move through this reflection.

Some years ago, as I read from the Biblical book of Isaiah, chapter 45, the image of the treasures of darkness caught my attention. In context, the Lord is speaking to Cyrus and telling of his victory that the Lord will make possible. Verses 2 and 3 in the NRSV read: "I will go before you and level the mountains, I will break in pieces the doors of bronze and cut asunder the bars of iron, I will give you the treasures of darkness and riches in secret places, so that you may know that it is I, the Lord, the God of Israel, who call you by your name."

In this reflection I am lifting the image, the treasures of darkness, out of its context. It caught my attention, and it is my intention here to use the image as a starting place to reflect on the experience of light and dark in Christian spirituality. My primary concern is for what I see as a split of darkness from light in the faith tradition. This can result in spiritual practices that are limited and even injurious to individuals and communities. The primary influence for my point of view is from the work of Carl Jung. Jung's concept of the Shadow is central to my reflection.

The split

Barbara Hannah, in *Encounters with the Soul*, makes this claim: "It was with the coming of Christianity that the white opposite alone was accepted, while the dark became more and more repressed and eventually was identified with the devil. It was a necessary development at the time, but it led to the repression of the personal shadow and to our present necessity of rediscovering it."[1]

Hannah asserts that this separation of light and dark was "a necessary development." As I think about it, I associate this with the natural development of our ego consciousness. As I understand it, from the beginning infants have no sense of separation from the mother. The separation develops over time and a sense of separate, continuous consciousness usually appears in early childhood. This sense of separation is "a necessary development." I remember years ago reading a small book by Paul Tournier entitled *Secrets*, in which he states that children around age eight become able to have secrets from their parents. He sees this as "a necessary development" for the individual. This sense of becoming a separate individual is essential to our ability to engage healthy relationships as life unfolds. My experience is that even in long-term relationships individuals remain to some degree separate and something of a mystery to each other. There is an important difference between being bonded to, or enmeshed with, another. Separation is a natural experience all through our lives; it is "a necessary development" that enables us to make distinctions between self and others, and to choose those qualities that shape who we are and how we will act. This natural process also constellates problems for us. One of these problems is the development of the Shadow, those other parts of us that we choose to repress and that form the unconscious content of the personal Shadow. The Shadow is a natural development that results from our choices in shaping our way of being in the world.

In my faith tradition this natural split is represented most clearly in the separation of the images of light and dark. In my experience we use images of light to represent or to convey the things of God, the holy and the good; and we tend to use images of darkness to represent that which is harsh, difficult, and even evil. This is the separation that Hannah observes as "a necessary development." It enables us in the collective community to choose the positive values and behaviours for our living together, and to repress and push down into the darkness of the unconscious those that we deem are negative. In most Christian spirituality and imagery, by identifying Christ with the Light exclusively, we create a collective Shadow out of the darkness, and require this darkness to carry the negative, the undesirable and what we see as evil. The Shadow exists for us in both personal and collective ways. Over time, and as "a necessary development," especially in our various faith traditions, light and dark have been separated in our worldviews into a polarized relationship of opposition and conflict. Out of our need to make decisions, distinctions, and choices for our living, we have repressed our less desirable impulses and urges into the Shadow. We split off these natural parts of us that do not fit the ideal. We relegate them to the Shadow and do our best to ignore them. This polarized, one-sided consciousness makes it almost impossible for us to see any problems with the light, and to appreciate the treasures of darkness. This polarization has had a substantial impact on our thinking and living. Darkness carries the negative that is to be avoided and light carries the positive way to be in the world. In my experience this thinking pervades my spiritual tradition and western culture at every turn and is reinforced in countless ways. As an archetypal "necessary development," this split seems primordial in human experience and predates our various Christian traditions and present cultures.

In this spiritual tradition we are caught in a polarized system of belief. Several passages from the NRSV translation of the Biblical texts demonstrate the dominant influence on our understanding and our spiritual practice. In John 8:12, Jesus declares: "I am the Light of the world; the one who follows me will not walk in darkness, but will have the light of life". This important and central image is expanded in 1 John 1:5-7: "… God is light and in him [sic] there is no darkness at all. If we say that we have fellowship with him [sic] while we are walking in darkness, we lie and do not do what is true;" This image is also put forth in James 1:17, wherein God is the "… Father of lights with whom there is no variation or shadow due to change." The writer of the Letter to the Ephesians, chapter 5:11, counsels his readers to "Take no part in the unfruitful works of darkness, but instead expose them."

The spiritual practice that results from this polarization of light and dark can drive us to focus relentlessly on those experiences, thoughts and feelings that are associated with the light. We will cling to positive and pleasurable experiences; we will seek peace and serenity and require ourselves and each other to try to be positive in most all instances. Likewise with some determination we may continue to push away the deep experiences of our hardships and sufferings, our grief's, disappointments and failings, and the normal difficulties of life. We may come to see these difficult times as somehow unnatural. Clinging to the light we often belittle and dismiss the reality of our struggles and can miss the valued lessons that may await us in what one man called the valleys of life. His statement to me was: "We learn more in the valleys than on the mountaintops." Many would feel guilt at even having to admit to these very natural human times, as if these experiences represent a failure of faith and trust in the Divine Life. It is not unusual for people living in this frame to suffer a life-long civil war in their souls between the light and dark experiences.

Psychically, this split, this state of civil war, leaves us polarized against ourselves. Far too many of us still live under the delusion that the best way to deal with our darker nature is through repression and avoidance. I remember speaking with a soft-spoken woman of faith many years ago who was very devoted to her Christian spiritual practice. She shared that she was traveling well except for the little gremlin who sat on her shoulder and sometimes whispered negative, critical thoughts in her ear. I asked her what she hoped to do with this gremlin, and she suddenly waved her arm over her shoulder and yelled, "Get outta here!" By these divisive practices of repression and avoidance we remain our own worst enemies. In such a divisive approach to the psyche, we obstruct our own path toward the fullness and wholeness of life offered to us through our relationship with the liberating and reconciling Divine Life. What began as "a necessary development," a natural separation of opposites for greater understanding and clarity, carries the potential to sever us from the treasures of darkness and from the fullness of ourselves, and to condemn us to narrow, one-dimensional lives.

Culturally, the polarized split of dark from light in many instances has had tragic influences on our common life. When we fuse what is good, righteous, and desirable with the light and the white, and assign what to us is bad, undesirable, and evil to the dark, we perpetuate the split. Our social structures naturally divide between what is good and light and what is bad and dark. In the face of this division, our capacity for diversity is diminished, and we push away as the undesirable "Other" those who are different. We inevitably take on values, images, practices, and form policies and structures that are degrading to people of colour. We tend to clothe our idealised images, our heroes, and heroines, including Jesus, in white. This simplistic idealisation was common in the visual images of the entertainment media in my younger years; good guys wear white, bad guys wear black. In identifying the light and white with goodness, with superior ways of living, and our desired virtues and with religious symbols, including the Christ image, we pave the way for people of colour in our midst, to carry the Shadow for the white community. As simplistic as it seems, in my lived experience it carries painful truth.

While I live in a more multicultural world than that of my childhood and youth, much of this tragic division remains present in the cultures of my experience. Black is most often equated with an inferior mentality and ability; it can be linked to being less able, dishonest, and violent. These are the qualities that compose the Shadow side of the light and white virtuous life. In terms of the gender issue in patriarchal societies, those negative qualities of darkness are most often expanded to include the feminine energy. This makes it possible and probable that women, as well, carry for white men and some women, the negative, dark Shadow of the chosen and dominant white culture. Women, as carriers of the feminine, are often seen in this paradigm as mysterious, conniving, secretive, manipulative, sneaky, and wily; persons who are out to disempower men if given the chance and who will mislead men from the path of the light and virtuous way. In the spiritual tradition, Eve's role in Adam's experience has often been cited as a precedent, as if the event was historical! We still miss the fact that without Eve, Adam would have never awakened to who he was. There is another whole mythological story here, not about a Fall, but about the birthing of human consciousness through the feminine, the natural birth-giver, and the ongoing creative and dynamic interaction that results between human consciousness and the larger divine life.

It is also important to note that the association of the colour black and the experience of darkness with holiness has a long history in Christian iconography. There is the brief mention in the Song of Solomon, chapter 1.5, wherein the speaker, perhaps the Queen of Sheba, declares, "I am black and beautiful."[2] The tradition of the Black Madonna is widespread throughout Europe with 400-500 representations. There has been little study of this iconic presentation and it is interesting to imagine how the number will increase when the research eventually encompasses the continent of Africa.[3]

Contemplating the Images

In the faith traditions and in our societies as well, we have been associating things negative with darkness and things positive with the light for a very long time. Therefore, reflecting on and valuing the treasures of darkness is a substantial challenge. It can be helpful to refresh our understanding with a brief review of some of the images of darkness and light.

Images of darkness that are positive include the darkness of the womb, that secret place of gestation and life, the source of birth, a lively and hidden place full of potential and creativity. It is interesting to note that in the tradition both the birth and the resurrection of Jesus took place in the dark, in the night. The sacred texts report that Jesus spent entire nights in prayer, and that Nicodemus came to visit him to talk in the night. We can imagine that the cave of Elijah was also dark and mysterious, not unlike a womb of sorts. The positive images include being out in the cool quiet of a dark night and being aware of the stillness and the silence. In those times we may have a sense of being enclosed in a place where our vision and perspective is often altered, and we can "see" more clearly with an inner eye. Such a night can be full of mystery, secrets, insights, and possibilities. It has all its own sounds and movements; it requires trust of oneself and trust of the larger life we sense around us that we cannot see. Darkness can be both intimate and cosmic in dimension. The darkness of the night offers us a different shape to our lives. In addition to the darkness of the landscape, we associate darkness with the ocean, that lovely, deep, great unknown that is full of life we cannot ordinarily see, like the mysterious unconscious that touches us all and is a vital, creative source of life.

In addition to land and the sea, there are positive experiences in the dark of honest, vulnerable conversations with someone close to us, and middle night conversations with parts of ourselves are often surprisingly honest. The darkness of night can also be a time of sexual connection that has a special magic. For many the darkness that surrounds us as we enter sleep is a welcome womb of stillness from the day's activity.

Laurens van der Post in *A Walk With A White Bushman*, offers a poetic description of the night as relief from the heat of the day and a time of renewal.[4] He reminds us also of the respite and comfort that comes with standing in the shade of a tree on a hot sunlit day. There is much about the darkness in our experiences that is positive.

Images of darkness that we experience as negative may seem more familiar to us. In the sacred tradition often the dark or darkness is that which we seek to avoid or overcome. Darkness is where the People walk until enlightened by the coming of the Christ. Christ is the light that darkness cannot overcome. We are encouraged to avoid the ways of darkness, to have nothing to do with the unenlightened. We are also told that some People prefer the ways of darkness to the ways of the light.

In terms of our psycho-spiritual experiences, in spite of the celebrated dark night of the soul put forward by St. John of the Cross,[5] we most often associate darkness with an ungodly experience. We speak of being in a dark or black mood, and in cultures with a rational bias, we are not inclined to welcome times of uncertainty or the darkness of mystery. This has been played out clearly in the present Covid pandemic across the globe. People are unnerved by our collective uncertain future; we fear losing our way, losing our daytime perspective. Many people have commented that these have been hard, dark times. Violence, aggression, and assault all are associated with a sense of darkness, as often are everyday stresses, tensions, and conflicts. In spiritual terms, darkness carries associations of ignorance, not understanding, being misled, being blind, being unconscious, and refusing to know. Implicit in all these associations is that darkness is closely associated with evil. The struggle against the darkness represented in these various experiences and images is the ongoing battleground in the Christian spiritual tradition.

Images of light that are positive are most common to us. In terms of landscape, we enjoy the warmth of the sun, sometimes after a cool dark night, or perhaps on a not too hot day. Light illumines the landscape so that we can appreciate its endless detail and remarkable life. Colours, textures, and shapes all come alive in landscape with the light.

In a psychospiritual frame the light helps us to see clearly – so much of this imagery has to do with seeing. It has to do with a clear perspective, accurate depth, and distance; realistic size and proportion; being able to identify what is there. The light is associated with finding and being found, with discovering, understanding, comprehending, accepting, and knowing. The light and consciousness are closely associated – enlightenment – and they include liberation and freedom. In the Biblical tradition we are informed of the positive light through the person, teaching, and the images of Jesus as the Christ. Our enlightenment through our faith teaches us that love, compassion and truth liberate us into being our best person.

The negative images of light are summarised for me in a teaching from childhood. We were taught never to look directly into the sun as it could blind us. Too much light becomes a serious threat to our wellbeing. We know from culture that too much sun, and too hot a climate is harmful to us. Moses could not look on the bright face of God and live, and later had to veil his face so that the light that shone from his countenance did not injure the People.

Too much. Marie-Louise von Franz claims Christians suffer from too much light. The darkness of the cave in Arizona obliterated our ability to see at all – too much darkness. While the separation begins as "a necessary development," too much light can blind us and too much darkness can also blind us. As we contemplate our associations with these images, it becomes clear that they are dangerous in their extreme forms. Too much of one or of the other can be injurious. As with the child in development, remaining enmeshed in an infantile attachment or radically separating out into a place of isolation are both damaging. All this may seem like an exercise in the obvious, but in a culture that still seems to interpret life through an either/or default position in many instances, it may be necessary to remind ourselves of the danger of too much light and of the treasures hidden away in the dark. If we can imagine a broad spectrum of light and dark then, it seems clear that our best position in somewhere between the two.

The challenge

Hannah asserts that the split between light and dark in the Christian tradition was "a necessary development" at the time. This split led to the development of the Shadow and its repression into the unconscious. She goes on to say that the necessary task in our time is to rediscover the Shadow. This is a core truth in both the individual life in reference to the personal Shadow and in reference to the collective Shadow in the Christian tradition and in our wider cultural, shared lives. The movement is from necessary split to necessary reunion. How do we bring polarized opposites of light and dark into their complementary dynamic once again? How do we acknowledge the dangers of too much light and embrace the treasures of darkness? What then must we do; what is the necessary work of the reunion of darkness and light in our own souls, in our faith traditions and in our cultures? So much in dominant cultures and faith traditions perpetuate the split and leaves us in danger of inner civil wars and outer tragic violent conflicts. How do we foster reunion? How do we heal the split?

Jung's understanding of the psyche and our collective life can help us find ways to engage and reconnect with this "other" life that is naturally a part of each of us and of our shared lives. Jung conceived of the psyche as having energies or qualities that exist in pairs of opposites. This he saw as our natural psychic state, and the natural movement in the psyche is to keep these complementary pairs of opposites in some sort of balance. In our early years at the knees of our elders, our character and world view begin to develop through their influences. Later we continue the process of our development based on what we have learned from our early elders and from our faith traditions and cultures. As we grow, we make choices between what is desirable and what is not. In this way we create the personal Shadow. Our positive choices become parts of our conscious perspective and we rarely are aware of how one-sided and limited our conscious points of view can be. The collective Shadow is created in groups that agree on what, or who, is acceptable and on who, or what, is not. Complementary opposites are split into conflicted opposites in this process of choosing. The qualities that we come to see as positive gain the focus of our attention and help form our conscious points of view; the other, its natural opposite is usually ignored, dismissed, or denied. This natural and almost automatic dynamic of choosing explains much of the unrest and interior warfare of the soul and our conflicts in our outer lives. For example, if we value and admire hard work, we tend internally to ignore the lazy one in us and are critical of those who do not seem to be pulling their weight. In recent years we collectively applied the terms "dole bludgers," and "leaners." Also, if we revere truth-telling, we tend to ignore the times when the other one hidden in us sneaks out as we rearrange the facts of an event or memory. We also will think badly of those who are caught out in significant fabrications in a more public forum.

To engage the Shadow requires us to reclaim the parts of us we have pushed away, and to withdraw our projections from those who have carried these rejected parts of our own souls. This presents an urgent and central ethic in the work of Jung. We are summoned to engage and include the Shadow in our renewed self-understanding. We are challenged to affirm the necessary and healing interplay between light and dark, Shadow and consciousness, in their varied individual and collective expressions. Our wholeness as individuals and the wellbeing of our faith traditions and our societies depend on this reunion.

It is important to affirm that the Shadow is not evil in and of itself, but simply is the natural psychic opposite of the image we present to the world as our conscious, public face. The Shadow is a psychic fact. It is not a problem to be solved, but a reality with which to live. While the shadow is not evil, it is that reality through which an evil impulse can easily slip, unaware and uninvited, into our lives. That which we deny and refuse to face, is independent of consciousness, and has a life of its own. This independent Shadow energy continues to seek recognition in order to strike the balance and create wholeness. We continue to push it away because our limited conscious minds usually perceive it as undesirable, dark and even evil. Pushing back against our repression, it struggles with consciousness for acknowledgement and/or expression. When thwarted, it finds ways to slip through into our words and actions, and we find ourselves saying and doing all manner of unexpected and untoward things. Another example of a Shadow experience is when we act suddenly out of character and then declare, "I don't know what came over me!" Perhaps we backpedal and say, "Oh, I didn't mean to say that!" What comes over us, what spills out of us, is the Shadow. In the extreme this escalates beyond mischief to violence, oppression, and destruction against the "Other" in both individual and collective ways.

To engage the Shadow means that we attribute value to this Other within at least because it is a legitimate part of who we are in our completeness. Our engagement may also include the realization that this Other within has qualities we need in order to express a more well-rounded life. In whatever way we understand this Other, we are naturally more whole and complete in ourselves simply by acknowledging and engaging this Other part of us.

To engage the Shadow does not mean that we must act it out. This is a secondary matter. Our acknowledgement within acts to expand our self-awareness of who we are. This acknowledgment then can enlarge our capacities for relationships with others, who are different and may be our "Others" as well. To engage those long-hidden Shadow parts of us also enables us to work to end the civil war in us between the diverse and sometimes oppositional attitudes and opinions in the soul. This can result in our being more compassionate to our struggling sisters and brothers.

However else we might imagine the Shadow it is also commonly seen as significantly golden. I see this image as having two aspects. First, the Shadow is gold because it contains what we need in order to live a more whole life. Some of these qualities may be negative by our conscious and cultural standards, but they can open us to a more rich, complex, and textured inner life, and some of these seemingly negative qualities may assist us to embody our ideals. Anger is yet another useful example. Many of us were trained early on to bury our capacity for anger in the Shadow. It was seen as undesirable, and an inappropriate response to life for mature and good people. Yet it may very well be the expression that we need in order to affirm ourselves, and to set appropriate boundaries as we move through a wounding experience. Anger can be golden.

Second, while our initial encounters with the images and energies of the Shadow will often be negative, the Shadow also holds dreams, hopes, and desires for a more creative life. These are positive and imaginative qualities that many of us set aside long ago because they were not practical, and our pursuit of them did not receive the approval of others. The gold can often be found in creative endeavours that will balance our everyday pursuits. They may even summon us to take up an entirely different path much to our surprise and the amazement of those who thought they knew us well. If we have the courage to embrace the fullness of who we are rather than live constricted one-dimensional lives, we will often find a richness, a diversity, and a completeness in ourselves. Engaging the "Other," the Shadow, often holds surprising treasures hidden in the darkness of our unconscious individual lives.

Engaging the Shadow within often has unexpected benefits for our relationships with others and for the common good. As we come to live more peacefully with ourselves through this spiritual discipline of Shadow work, we enlarge our capacities to interact creatively with people who are different both in cultural fashion and skin pantone. We can find ourselves able to be more open to those whose visions for life, opinions on social process, and involvements in cultural rituals and beliefs are significantly different from ours. Engaging the Shadow enables us to create and nurture deep and sustainable communities with diverse peoples. We are enriched and enlarged and more whole as a People. If we do not do this, if we do not risk engaging the treasured darkness of ourselves, we risk contributing to the collective Shadows of our preferred groups that will develop and support destructive attitudes and actions toward the "Other." Our recent collective history offers too many examples. Violent encounters around gender, ethnic and skin colour tensions are the result of collective Shadow energies breaking out. National conflicts, clashes over faith traditions, and abuses of minority groups all spring from the collective Shadow of dominant and dominating groups.

Together

Our consideration of the images of light and dark invite us, summon us, to reflect on the interaction of the two. In fact, they are essential to one another. We need the darkness to appreciate the functions of the light; we need the light to understand the blessings of the dark. Shadows keep light from being flat, indeed the Shadow keeps life from being flat. Without our Shadows, life will look very much like a polar bear in a snowstorm.

With some disciplined self-reflection, we realise we experience the two together in natural ways. There is the magic of a campfire outside in the night. Lighted candles and the stars are best seen in the dark. Standing in the shade on a sunny day is a great relief and pleasure. Flickering sunlight through branches of a tree create lively shadows. The interplay of the two is like the mandorla; that almond shaped, numinous centre created when two opposite circles intersect, and in the overlay, create an integrated space that is sacred by virtue of being composed of both circles. The numinous magic of the interaction of the dark and light is seen daily at both sunrise and sunset. Toss in some clouds that take on colours from the rays of the rising or setting sun, and the moments vibrate with a larger life in which we live.

An image that is often a container for the treasures of darkness is the abyss. Perhaps as endless as the image of abyss is, so are the implications of it for us. For me the image of the abyss became alive during a series of active imagination dialogues beginning in 1977 and continuing into 1979. I came to the abyss down winding stone stairs being led in the dark by a Great Dane dog. Over time I went deeper into my underworld to this abyss which extended bottomless into dark vast space. In the abyss was "no-thing"; it was not nothing, but "no-thing." The abyss was alive, vibrant, with life. The top of the abyss was like a dome shaped ceiling, through which protruded many tube-like structures. Through these tube-like structures, the "no-thing" life entered the world of particularity. Some tubes were long, large, and clear; others were small and twisted and little of the "no-thing" life was able to move through them. Such was the passing of the "no-thing" through the tubes, that the particularities that carried "no-thing" often bore no resemblance to one another. But at the heart of the abyss all was One. There was no sense of light in the abyss, but the darkness of the abyss was not a crushing darkness, only what was. In a sense it was a darkness in which one would "see," if there was anything to see! But in the abyss, there was nothing to do, but simply to be. The deeper I went along the abyss cavern, the wider the abyss became, and the quieter it was. At first my Great Dane dog was my guide, and then the Christ guided me, and at the lowest level to which we went, even Christ sent me on alone to sit on a single chair, on a narrow bridge, across the vast abyss. There, in the darkness of the abyss, I sat silently in the presence of "no-thing," who was All, the One. Such was my experience of the abyss. The realisation that became clear in that dark place is simply that at the heart of it all, all is One. In that dark underworld I found treasures, insights, but also treasures in the form of people. They are the raggle-taggle people who make up my inner village. Some are wise, remarkable, and creative, and some are rather wild and strange with whom I deal carefully. In the darkness these treasures contribute to my wholeness; they enlighten me and expand my capacity to live peacefully within, and compassionately with others. Joseph Campbell, in his interviews with Bill Moyers in *The Power of Myth*, makes this assertion: "One thing that comes out of myths is that at the bottom of the abyss comes the voice of salvation. The black moment is the moment when the real message of transformation is going to come. At the darkest moment comes the light."[6]

Conclusion

While at some point in our lives we need to separate light and dark in order to appreciate both, the integration of the two in their natural state is an essential goal. This is true of the individual soul and of our collective groupings. The interplay of light and dark is numinous, and archetypal, the manifestation of mandorla. All of these mandorla images and experiences are symbols and expressions of the holy, and of the possible completeness of being for which we ache in the secret places of our souls. The recovery of the treasures of darkness presents us with the possibilities of expanding our lives beyond the usual one-sidedness of consciousness, to a more rounded out, potentially complete sense of self, and of the potential completeness of others as well. It presents us with the possibility of the fullness of life about which Jesus spoke in Biblical book of John. Further, and most importantly, to revalue the dark, and to respect the light means that we might come to that place where we are no longer inclined to project our unlived or denied lives within out onto others. It is possible to come to a place in this life where we no longer need to scapegoat and blame others, a place in which we no longer need enemies, where we are able to live in peace with ourselves, and in this way finally become people who create and cultivate peace. The treasures of darkness are integrated with the treasures of light, and we relax into the completeness of our lives. It is possible.

Endnotes

1. Hannah, Barbara. *Encounters with the Soul.* p. 27.
2. The Song of Solomon, *The Holy Bible*, NRSV. Oxford University Press. p. 691, Chapter 1, vs 5.
3. The Black Madonna, in Wikipedia. The article refers to the research of Ean Begg. 2017. *The Cult of the Black Virgin*. Chiron Publications.
4. van der Post, Laurens. *A Walk with A White Bushman.* p. 10.
5. Along with John of the Cross, there are exceptions in the faith Tradition in which darkness is seen as positive and necessary experience. Two recent reflections came to me while completing this essay. That they should arrive during this time I take as remarkable examples of synchronicity. A friend in Portland, Oregon, sent the first. It is a poem by David

Whyte entitled "Sweet Darkness" from his collection, *The House of Belonging*, 2010. A colleague in South Africa, sent the second. It is a reflection from the daily internet reflections from Richard Rohr, 29 December 2021, from the Center for Action and Contemplation. In this Rohr presents the work of Barbara Holmes, an African American woman. It is entitled "The Wisdom of Darkness" and is excerpted from her work, *Crisis Contemplation: Healing the Wounded Village*.

6. Campbell, Joseph. *The Power of Myth*. p. 37.

References

Campbell, Joseph, with Moyers, Bill. 1988. Betty Sue Flowers. Ed. *The Power of Myth*. New York: Doubleday.

Hannah, Barbara. 1981. *Encounters with the Soul: Active Imagination as Developed by C. G. Jung*. New York: Sigo Press.

van der Post, Laurens. 1986. *A Walk with A White Bushman*. London: Penguin Books.

Empowerment from within:
Listening to the soul

I delivered the following talk at a conference entitled, "Women! Choice! and the 21st Century!" It was held at Notre Dame University, in Fremantle, Western Australia, on 18 September 1998. I was surprised and honoured to be the only male invited to address the day-long conference. I was asked to focus on the contributions of depth psychology in reference to empowerment for women. Inevitably, I have edited the original notes in reformatting them for this present reflection.

Introduction

I am grateful for the opportunity to speak at today's symposium and am mindful of the fact that I am a man speaking about women, almost exclusively to women. As I understand it, I have been invited along to bring a particular perspective to our topic for the day: Women! Choice! and the 21st Century! My perspective on most things is deeply influenced by the work of Carl Jung, and today is no exception. Therefore, I intend to reflect on the notion of empowerment from within, and working from a perspective influenced by Jung's work, will reflect on four dreams and one meditation experience, all shared with me by women over the years. I hope these reflections will be useful to you. Let's begin with Madeline's dream.

Madeline's dream: A very complete person

It's daylight – maybe early morning or early evening. I am on my bed looking out through the fly wire at the back of the sleep out and I see a rough tin shelter adjoining the laundry. It is only about a metre high. In this shelter is a little girl, about age 8, dressed in the period of the mid to late 19th century. Her dress is tan to brown, and she is wearing a mop cap. Next to her on her left are a calf and a lion cub.

Madeline presented this dream to me when she was in her late 50s. She had the dream experience when she was about six years old and had carried it with her for over fifty years. Madeline's memory of the time of the dream was that she was very anxious and frightened, and she notes that the fear still visits her sometimes now. She was a child during the years of the Second World War and has come to realise that in her home there was an undercurrent of anxiety and fear because of the war, and these affected her very deeply. She was the eldest of four girls and carried a deep sense of responsibility for her younger siblings. She makes the following statement as part of her brief reflection on this dream.

"The little girl didn't speak but she wasn't afraid. In fact, as I look back and with the benefit or otherwise of life's experiences, my feeling about this child is that she was and is a very complete person."

I remember reading in a magazine, during this last year, a comment made by Germaine Greer. She remarked that she had a clearer sense of herself at about age eleven than at any other age in her life. It was her opinion that once a young girl becomes a sexual person at puberty her own agenda is hijacked by the expectations of her society. Such are the socialising pressures on women, that it is difficult to regain that simple clarity of self. In the dream the little girl, with the calf and the lion cub, is not afraid, and appears to be "a very complete person."

Today we owe a great debt of gratitude to the disciplines of psychology for helping us recover the dream as a vital resource for guidance and self-understanding. Carl Jung is among the leaders in this field, whose approach to dreams I have used as part of my own spiritual practice for many years. A primary characteristic of dreams is that they often seek to compensate for the limited perspective of consciousness. In part that is the function of Madeline's dream. Even as a child she was anxious and frightened, and these feelings have affected her adversely all throughout her life. Yet she has never forgotten the dream of the little girl who was not anxious and frightened. The image compensates for the anxieties and fears of her childhood and is a constant reminder of another way, another vital aspect of her own being.

At a deeper level the dream speaks a sacred truth. We in the Christian tradition can hardly miss the sacred imagery of the picture: the child and the animals at peace. This imagery is grounded in the writings of the prophet Isaiah and connected by the Christian people to the Christ. Here in the dream of a frightened six-year-old girl, we see a compensatory female Christ child image, a child who is not afraid, one who appears as "a very complete person."

In our theological language we speak variously of the image of God and the God within. Matthew Fox has challenged us to think about original blessing, Jung speaks of original wholeness, James Hillman uses the acorn seed as an image of the soul coming to birth and fulfilling its destiny in life. Whatever image we use, this dream invites us to reflect on the possibility of a centre of truth and of strength deep within us, who is present from the beginning. This deep centre within contains the sense of being "a very complete person," whose presence is a source of strength, encouragement, and empowerment. It is a primary task in our lives to bring her to fruition.

Madeline's dream and Germaine's remark invite women to affirm the truth that from the very beginning we are each "someones." Within us there is a vital centre of personal identity that is godly, Christly, sacred, and substantial. Even the social-sexual expectations of our society cannot take this from us.

Over the years of my work, I have listened to many women in the various settings of counselling, spiritual direction, and psychotherapy. I conclude that we do in fact socialise women to be referential persons, and to see their fulfillment largely in what they do for others, usually for spouses and children, sometimes for parents, the church and other communities of people in need. I cannot remember how many women have told me that it seems selfish to spend even a little time thinking about themselves. It is as if self-care for women was a sin. Worse, I have seen others who seem to have no idea of who they are in themselves, or what they want, or what their destinies might be, except in serving others. They seem to exist only in reference to others, and too often this vacuous sense of self is somehow seen as a positive picture of Christian piety. I recognise that I speak in generalities, but I believe these contain some truth. As part of this I want here to affirm that the roles of mother and wife are sacred in their own rights and worthy of our deepest respect. This is also true of roles women undertake outside the home, whether as volunteers or in the paid workforce. The sacred nature of women's varied roles are all inclusive. I am not convinced that women must settle for a referential sense of self to perform any of these functions successfully.

Madeline's dream raises the issue of a sense of self. The affirmation of a strong sense of self, one that is self-referential, is a primary task for women as we continue into the 21st century. It is my conviction that affirming, protecting, and exploring the self-vision of childhood as identified by Germaine Greer is an essential task for women in their search for sacred self-fulfilment.

Such undertakings are fraught with the dangers of narcissistic self-indulgence. Narcissism seems to be a destructive threat in our present generations. Yes, there is always the possibility that women might become as self-absorbed as are many of us men! Such dangers are easily avoided when we envision our life task of developing a strong sense of self in the wider context of the eternal Christ of God. My understanding of the Christ way is that we who struggle to develop a strong self-referential sense of self, and who are grounded in a vision of truth from within, are then able to make significant contributions in countless ways for the Common Good.

From Jung's work we learn that the dream is a primary resource in the development of a strong self-referential sense of self. One of the results of listening to our dreams is that we begin to realise that we have a speaking centre of truth within us, a voice of wisdom who nightly guides us in the unfolding of our lives. These sacred stories, speaking a symbolic language, challenge us with the ongoing tasks of our unfolding lives. These dreams, often presented in wonderful, curious, and complex images, comment on the issues that need our attention. They also may give us insight as we seek to share our truth from within into our larger communities. Such is Ann's dream.

Ann's dream: The Green snake

I am a young woman and I live in a little house in the forest with an older woman, who is lovely, serene, about 30 and non-aggressive. She wears a lace cap, and other old-fashioned clothes. Her body is not visible, only her lovely face.

But there is some threat to us from people from an organisation close by, where I also worked. We didn't have any personal power, but the idea of the green snake seemed first to be given to us; we accepted, overjoyed, as it was a way, once and for all, to escape from and overcome the patriarchal male organisation which kept us prisoner.

We were given the opportunity to watch the green snake be born; it was just about 6 inches long. We saw it with some awe and such joy, and then it slithered off to safety until it grew into full power. It went into trees and woods that were near our house so that the organisation couldn't find it. They wanted to find it and kill it; they didn't believe it was a magical snake with strong powers. They were frightened of it and sent a security guard to be on guard at our house at all times; they would change shifts. I locked and bolted the door with three locks so that they couldn't come in, and we would have our privacy with the snake when it came to dinner. I set the table with flowers and candles to make it beautiful for the snake. When the security guards saw it, they couldn't believe that one would do this for a snake. They wondered why I held it in such esteem. By this time, it had grown into a big green snake. With this support from the snake, we achieved freedom from the organisation, and some respect.

We could spend a long time with this dream. For Ann it was a turning point in her life. In her own reflections she described it as going back and doing life all over again. The dream recognises that, for many women, there has been something imprisoning about the present society. Here it is called the "patriarchal male organisation." Ann realised that she did in fact work for the organisation, and that she, like countless other women, had been complicit in her own imprisoning. She knew no other way. But then came the green snake.

The snake image is a gift: "the idea of the green snake seemed first to be given to us; we accepted, overjoyed, as it was a way, once and for all, to escape from and overcome the patriarchal male organisation which kept us prisoner." Ann and her companions saw the green snake born. She described in later reflection how she and her companions were joined by several angelic beings. They formed a circle and watched as the snake seemed to emerge from among the leaves on the forest floor. It was an awesome sight. Once again, we sense the sacred overtones around this image. While the dominant attitude toward the snake in the Judeo-Christian tradition is hardly positive – the Garden of Eden and all that – in another perspective in our own tradition, and in other religious traditions, including the Australian Aboriginal religious traditions, the snake carries much sacred importance and is connected to the coming of life and creativity.

Ann's dream stresses the truth that women have access to sacred resources of life and creativity within their own souls by way of the unconscious. In the Christian tradition we speak about the experience of the gift of grace. Here in this dream, we recognise that same notion of a graced gift. Jung saw that the unconscious was a vital resource of creativity. For Jung, entering a dialogue with the unconscious by listening to our dreams and other impulses from within, gives us wonderful gifts.

The dialogue with the unconscious over time Jung names as the process of individuation, wherein we each learn who we are in our uniqueness, and who we are meant to be in our shared lives with others. For Jung, the journey of individuation is a sacred journey. Many of us might not have an image of a green snake who we respect and invite for dinner, for our symbols are tailor-made for each of us by the spirit of the unconscious who creates the dream stories. For Ann it was a vital and life-giving image, and her attentiveness to this dream and to the snake in her subsequent imaginal experiences, assisted her significantly in becoming free from the prison in which she had lived for many years.

For Jung, the journey of individuation is a religious journey, whether it involves us in an organised religious group or not. For us in the Christian tradition, Jung's process becomes a useful tool for accessing the rich and wonderful gifts of the unconscious that contribute to our unfolding lives. For women, Ann's dream demonstrates that the unconscious is a rich resource for the empowerment of women against whatever has imprisoned them. The key is to have the courage to listen to the dream. Clare's dream demonstrates the need for courage even more clearly.

Clare's dream: Broken glass and son's journey

I am helping my twenty-year-old son organise his last few days at home before he leaves to go away – overseas or at least a long way from here. I have done what I can and what has been appropriate, but it is not my task to actually take him to the airport or collect up his luggage. We go to the place where we are to meet his father, from whom I am divorced.

When we walk in, or come into the place, I find that nothing at all is in order or ready to be put into the car to leave. In fact, the luggage isn't even there: it is still back in another place and not even packed. This was his father's responsibility. Not only that, but his dad is sitting around with a bunch of other men, all old friends of his and what I would call smug types, comfortable, smug, content with their own views of the world ... they are sitting around drinking (not drunk, just socialising) as if there is nothing else happening.

I cannot believe it: this is the most important event in my son's life so far – his leaving for this major and important trip – and none of them seem to have the slightest idea of the magnitude, and none of them have bothered to do anything or make any kind of effort.

At this point I step completely out of my 'character' or usual way of behaving. Instead of being reasonable, and trying to persuade them to do something, or (as I could well do) do it myself so that it does actually happen, I lose it completely. I scream, shout, and get angrier than I have ever been before. I grab a wine glass, and threaten the men with it, with absolute menace: I tell them that if they don't get their acts together right now, I will break the glass and go for them ... they are amazed and don't believe me because I have always been such a nice, reasonable, and undemanding person. But soon they begin to see that I am serious: that I really will go for them with broken glass. My rage is enormous.

As we might easily imagine, Clare was unnerved by her dream. To express such violent rage clearly was stepping out of her usual character. Yet in the dream it seems there was no other way to make her point. For her much was at stake. The image of the travels of the young son was intimately connected to her own development as a whole person. Too long the male influences in her life had not taken her seriously, had not cooperated with her attempts to unfold into the fullness of her divinely given self. In her desperation she was driven to discover the life-giving rage within her.

One of the key characters of the inner world that Jung identifies is the Shadow. The Shadow in us is the one who carries all the "other" aspects of us, those qualities that we have not developed, that we've been told to put away, or have deliberately pushed aside, of which we are ashamed or embarrassed, and which cause discomfort or even fear in our consciousness. In itself, the Shadow is not evil, but it can feel menacing to our carefully constructed conscious pictures of ourselves, and its presence can sometimes leave us shaken and surprised, as it also might do to the people around us when it emerges. We often might wonder, "Where did she come from?" We usually experience our Shadow moments as entirely outside our usual, conscious character.

The challenge of Clare's dream is the challenge of emotional honesty. Clare is reminded again by this dream of the importance of being honest with her feelings about the circumstances through which she is living. Such honesty often involves acknowledging this Shadow side of us. This acknowledgment may cause us discomfort, but it spares us the useless exercise of pretending to be people we are not. Rather than wasting energy in maintaining a self-concept that is untrue, we are liberated to use our energies more wisely for the unfolding of our lives and destinies.

In her work, *Women at the Well: Feminist Perspectives on Spiritual Direction*, Kathleen Fischer, referring to work by Fran Ferder asserts that anger "was purposefully and lovingly created and shaped by God as a source of energy, as a source of fire."[1] Anger, a revelation of God, a source of divine fire, an aspect of God's own being, what strange notions these are to the minds and hearts of women socialised to be reasonable and civil at all costs. The challenge is emotional honesty, even if this causes us much discomfort and requires us to rearrange our self-understanding. The benefit is to tap into a deep life-giving energy that assists us in the wholesome unfolding of our lives. Clare's dream affirms that our confrontation with the Shadow demands courage. The confrontation may also hold surprises for us as Effie's dream reveals.

Effie's Dream: Diving in to swim with fish

A Woman is fishing from the deck of a big sailing boat. I have never seen this woman before. She looks relaxed as she stands with her line over the railing. She has black hair, seems rather sophisticated, and is wearing a raincoat over her dress. She looks very feminine.

A big fish appears in the water below. She sees it and it sees her. The sea is quite rough. Not wanting to catch the fish, which is too big anyway, she suddenly dives into the water and is close enough to put her arms around the fish. There is warmth and affection between the pair as they play. Meanwhile, a man on board the boat is watching all this and says, "I suppose I'd better go in after her. There are probably sharks out there!" Annoyed and reluctant, he dives in and, just as he hits the water, black fins appear, and he fears the worst.

But a school of dolphins appear and surround the woman who is playing ecstatically with the fish in calm, almost shallow water.

It has been some years since I met with Effie to discuss her dreams, but I still remember her infectious laughter, and what a laugh she had over this story. The woman on the ship was a stranger to her, and she was not at all like her. Here is an example of what is called the "golden" shadow. What Effie saw in this woman was the courage to take a risk and jump, which was not Effie's usual conscious orientation to life. She, too, had been influenced negatively by a certain aspect of the masculine voice. He had undermined her confidence and left her feeling timid in her aspirations for her own life.

The woman is fishing, doing honest work as Robert Johnson says, reaching into the great unconscious life for some nourishment. She sees the great fish and takes the risk. In she jumps, in spite of the rough sea! The fish is an ancient symbol of the Christ, so there is something sacred about this undertaking. Despite the reservations and fears of the man who is watching, the woman is safe, and she and the fish are circled by playful dolphins. The circle is a simple sign of the completeness of things, and the dolphin another sign of the Christ. All up, the woman made a solid decision to take the leap.

Effie's dream encouraged her to believe that she had the courage within her to take the risk, the leap, when life presented significant opportunities. She could do it and do it well. For women, adversely influenced by negative male voices and opinions, the challenge is to believe, first, that she can perceive the opportunity as it is given, and second that the courage to act successfully is within her. The golden shadow is that yet to be discovered aspect of us who represents the positive energies we need, so that we can embrace the challenges of our lives. The discovery of this one within is often a process of great joy as we undertake adventures hitherto thought to be beyond the scope of our abilities.

These reflections raise an interesting notion concerning sin. Ann Ulanov in her work, *Receiving Woman*, affirms that "for a woman sin is not pride, an exaltation of self, but a refusal to claim the self God has given."[2]

The man was wrong, the woman was right to jump, and all ended safely and in joy. She was right to trust herself and take the risk. For Effie the dream challenges her to realise that there is a sacred quality about this leaping, this risk taking. In her story a relationship with Christ, with God is implied throughout. Helen's experience brings this issue more clearly into focus.

Helen's story

Helen had come to me for some time for spiritual direction. She was a woman of considerable depth whose practice of contemplation took her to deep and quiet places of the soul. One day at the beginning of a week she came to see me and was agitated. I asked her what was up, and she told me of her meditation experience on the weekend. In a time of quiet she had gone deep within and had realised while there that the only way to describe the presence she met was not as "he," but as "she." She was upset, a little frightened and not sure how to proceed. Helen was a life-long Christian, and in spite of her discomforts with the institutional church, she believed deeply in the Christ event and story. What to do?

I remind us, as we hear Helen's story, that the Christ figure in Madeline's dream was a little girl. These images from the unconscious invite women to consider how they are placed cosmologically. The issue has to do with God.

In the Christian tradition men have had little difficulty finding their place cosmologically, it is grounded in the male imagery of the divine life. Kathleen Fischer points out that women have always been translating the gender imagery to their own experience. The substantial contribution of Christian women in the feminist tradition is to challenge us to re-think our God imagery. The body of literature is large and growing and deserves our careful attention and respect. Maternal and feminine imagery for God not only arises from the unconscious, as in Helen's case, but is actually a part of the scriptural tradition as Virginia Mollenkott points out in her work, *The Divine Feminine*.[3] In considering the feminine and maternal in God, we are not then re-inventing Christian imagery, we are simply paying attention to that which has been there all along. While a careful consideration of this issue may take us to places of thought we have not been before, our journey begins with a careful re-reading of our own familiar, sacred texts.

For women, the issue means affirming that their own nature is grounded in the divine life from the very beginning. Women are placed equally to men in the cosmos by virtue of the image of God. Today as we carry with us our hopes for societies that truly are gender equal, we have the great opportunity to ground our hopes in the gender-inclusive imagery of God from the beginning of creation. For women, this affirms a very different place to stand cosmologically. The 'presence' in the depths of women and men, the 'one' who meets Helen and any of us in the quiet moments of contemplation, meditation, and prayer, is both she and he, according to our need. Though Jesus of Nazareth was in fact a male, the eternal Christ of God may appear to us as girl or boy, woman, or man in the soul's imagery. This truth empowers women as does no other, for it places her as truly equal to men in the cosmological story.

Conclusion

These are both exciting and frightening times. A great joy for women today is to learn increasingly about the empowerment that comes from within. Jung helps us see the dream as a vital resource for this process. From the dreams and the story, we have considered briefly today we are reminded of significant insights for women as we move along.

1) Women carry within themselves, from the beginning, a sense of self that is sacred, whose unfolding is one of the primary tasks of life.
2) The unconscious, the giver of the dreams, offers many gifts for the unfolding of our lives. Like gifts of grace in the religious tradition, unconscious energies come forward to contribute significantly to the unfolding of that acorn like self, known from earliest days.
3) Along with gifts, the unconscious offers challenges, including the challenge to acknowledge the raging Shadow and the challenge to claim the courage to reach out and embrace the person we are called to become.

4) All of this happens in the larger framework of women finding their places cosmologically, by finding themselves in the gender-equal images of the divine energies, which are at the core of all our searching, and the central energy of all our hopes. The challenge then is to build together social structures grounded in justice, compassion, equality, and love. Helped in our understanding by Jung, it is not idle to hope that our dreams may well come true. Thanks to the five women who allow me to share their experiences and I thank you for your attention.

Endnotes

1. Fischer, Kathleen. *Women at the Well.* pp 179–80.
2. Ulanov, Ann. B. *Receiving Woman.* p. 134.
3. Mollenkott, Virginia. *The Divine Feminine.*

References

Fischer, K. (1988). *Women at the Well: Feminist Perspectives on Spiritual Direction. London*: SPCK.

Mollenkott, V. (1984). *The Divine Feminine: The Biblical Imagery of God as Female.* New York: The Crossroad Publishing Company.

Ulanov, Ann B. (1981). *Receiving Woman: Studies in the Psychology and Theology of the Feminine.* Philadelphia: The Westminster Press.

Spirituality and Psychotherapy

The original talk was delivered on 2 March 2000, to the Psychotherapists and Counsellors Association of Western Australia. At the time I functioned as the University Chaplain at Edith Cowan University, as well as continuing my Analytical Therapy practice and my work as an artist. I had recently completed my PhD thesis entitled, "Active Imagination and Christian Religious Experience: A Study in Relationship," and was awarded my degree later in the same year. I acknowledge that some of my perspectives have shifted over the years and that I have made some changes for clarity. In-text references in the original document have been re-formatted as endnotes.

Introduction

Over the months during which I have reflected on this topic, I have concluded that it is inappropriate to contrast these two areas of experience in some simplistic way. It isn't a matter of one or the other, spirituality or psychotherapy. I do understand that for some in various religious communities it might still be a matter of one or the other. There are still some in my Christian tradition who believe that problems are to be addressed by the faithful in prayer, and not by seeking psychological help. Too many times over the years I have heard people of some sort of faith dismiss psychology outright. Conversely, I remember a client telling me that when she introduced her faith into the discussion with a former counsellor, she was told clearly that the religion had nothing to do with the counselling agenda at hand. So, for some, these two areas are exclusive, but not for me and I hope not for you. To begin with, then, I affirm that spirituality and psychotherapy are related. These two areas do not stand in opposition to one another; they are not a pair of conflicted opposites. An exercise of comparison that divides them is not appropriate.

To help me reflect on these two areas of experience I have framed several questions for consideration.

> What is the role of spirituality in psychotherapy?
> Is psychotherapy a spiritual exercise?
> Does it contain elements of spirituality?
> What has psychotherapy to do with religion?
> How does spirituality relate to psychotherapy?

With these in mind I have shaped a reflection for this evening. My method, as usual, leans on the work of Dr Carl Jung and the style of circumambulation, that is, walking around in a topic. My intention here is to consider several topics, and I hope we each will leave here with a useful understanding as to how spirituality and psychotherapy are related.

Spirituality: A Definition

As we begin, let me first define spirituality. This task first became a part of my conscious concerns just over twenty years ago, when I was asked to develop a regional study program for the training of spiritual directors in the United States. This was in conjunction with Alan Jones, who was then on the faculty of The General Seminary in New York City and the Director of the Centre for Christian Spirituality there. He was then for years the Dean of Grace Cathedral in San Francisco. My present definition of spirituality has grown out of our work together.

Spirituality is the art of making and discovering connections. The connections are fourfold. The first is with the transpersonal reality, the Divine Other or with whatever we mean by God; the second is with ourselves; the third is with those around us who make up our personal worlds; the fourth is with the larger world community, and indeed, all of creation. In short: God, self, others, world. On the one hand, these connections are made by our own efforts. On the other hand, we discover them to be part of our lives through our reflections. This latter discovery connects to what Christians refer to as "grace." Making and discovering reflect the age-old pair of complementary opposites in the religious traditions of effort and grace. Some things we do; others seem to happen for us.

When I hear talk of spirituality, it often has to do with activity or practices. Spirituality is concerned with the practices I undertake to make or discover connections. While this is an emphasis, I would suggest that spirituality also contains some sense of a theoretical understanding or faith about God, self, others, and world, otherwise one would have no framework in which to act, no motivating factor to fuel action. In short, I maintain that we all believe something about Other, self, others, and the world, however unconscious or critiqued this may be. In a time when institutional religions are not as attractive as they once were, many may be aware of what they don't believe, but less aware of what it is that they do believe and of what fuels the fires and passions of spirituality.

Having said this, I affirm that the primary dynamic of spirituality is activity. Spirituality is primarily focussed on practices that make for the connections. Spirituality here has to do with wellbeing. The practices we undertake are meant to facilitate some sense of meaningful and satisfactory connection to whatever the Other or divine energy, is for us. They are also to assist in how I keep connected to myself, my feelings, attitudes, and responses to experiences, and how I maintain connections to the people, the others, who make up my everyday world. Finally, these are practices that help me place myself in the larger human family and in the creation. Let me add here that, while our connection to the creation is listed last of the four, it is not to imply that it is the least important. From my theological point of view, the contemporary issues around the feminine images of the deity, the recovery of soul, the development of a spiritual ecology, and responses to the environmental issues of our time, all involve this fourth dimension of our spiritualities. Briefly then, while any spirituality is grounded in a perspective on life or a belief system, however conscious or unconscious, spirituality is also a series of activities and practices that we undertake to cultivate a sense of wellbeing.

The definition of spirituality I have offered is meant to be inclusive. In this context, I affirm that all people live in some sort of spiritual framework. It is a definition that we place within whatever theory or belief system works for the individual. Mine for instance is the Christ story. So, my spirituality is a Christ-centred spirituality. I hasten to add that this does not mean that I have an undying and uncritical commitment to institutional Christianity.

From my point of view, there is considerable overlap at this point between spirituality and psychotherapy. As I understand my work in psychotherapy, I am deeply concerned with the spirituality of the client, that is, with how the client makes and discovers essential connections that help counteract or heal some of the alienating wounds of life, and the isolation that often results from those wounds. I am concerned with how the individual enacts practices that rebuild and strengthen those connections. I am concerned with the overall wellbeing of the client. From my point of view, whatever its clinical base, psychotherapy is an exercise that is infused with spirituality. It suits my personal framework to affirm that psychotherapy has all the hallmarks of a sacred process. Having now defined spirituality, I want to turn my attention to the notions of spiritual experience and religious experience.

Reflections on Spiritual Experience and Religious Experience

My reflections here are based on a section of my recently submitted PhD thesis entitled, *"Active Imagination and Christian Religious Experience: A Study in Relationship."* During my research, I found it necessary to reflect on the relationship between spiritual and religious experiences. In early 1996, as I began my research project, I was talking to a friend about the subject of my research. When I mentioned Christian religious experience, he immediately responded that I should change it to "spiritual" experience. He further commented that he felt done with religion but was very interested in spirituality. In my experience, the distinction my friend made is relatively recent in the general conversations in our culture, but it is no longer uncommon. How might we distinguish between religious and spiritual experience? If psychotherapy has to do with spirituality, has it to do also with religion? While this topic interests me greatly, I admit at the outset that I have no satisfactory or final understanding as to how to distinguish between religious and spiritual experiences. What I offer here are reflections towards an understanding. First, I present a reflection of David Tacey's, and second, parts from the taped interview conversations I shared with Morton Kelsey in January 1998. Kelsey is my mentor for some forty years, and a pioneer in the American scene in bridging Christian theology and Jungian psychology. As I begin here, I remind us that Alan Jones' definition of spirituality affirms that all people have a spirituality, which can be placed within the context of a belief framework.

At the Australian New Zealand Society of Jungian Analysts (ANZSJA) Conference in Melbourne, February 1997, at LaTrobe University, David Tacey remarked that the categories of the spiritual and religious were seen, until recently, to be identical and to be the prerogative of the church. He maintained that only in recent times have we begun to separate the two. Tacey has seen this happen with students at the university and others. There are those who are developing a reverential attitude toward a larger life without being involved in the religious enterprise. For Tacey then, "spiritual" refers to this reverential attitude toward life in a broad sense. "Religious" focuses this attitude through a faith response to the gods.

During the taped conversations I had with Kelsey, we entered a discussion of the distinctions between spiritual and religious. At first, he asserted that these are different experiences. When I pushed him for distinctions, he responded in a somewhat disjointed manner, "One is organised, that's a bad word, one is the concretised religious with the historical setting … religious search within the historical setting."[1] We agreed that the religious might involve an historical setting while the spiritual seems to begin with a less clear and predisposed framework. We pushed on and then Kelsey stated, "I would say that the deepest form of Christianity is a form of both deep religion and deep spirituality." We talked for some time trying to align religious experience more with creeds and dogmas and organised religions and trying to see spiritual experiences as more clearly aligned with a concern for direct experience apart from organised religious structures. The distinction felt a bit simplistic and forced. Kelsey then talked about his recent work of revising one of his books. He confessed: "We purposefully, probably to avoid this very problem, would not confine ourselves to one word for the divine, the spiritual, God, … that it is a multi-faceted jewel … If we could, I would say, if we could link the words together, spiritual-religious, so it is a double word. All the nuances of the spiritual can't be covered in one word." In the remainder of our conversations, we decided to hyphenate the words. We spoke of things as spiritual-religious to demonstrate to ourselves their connection. Jones, Tacey and Kelsey form a background as I walk around in this topic. Here are several points to consider.

First, I agree with Tacey that the distinction is recent. The world in which I grew up would have seen all things spiritual as religious and would have believed that these were the business of the organised religions. I do think that sweeping changes in recent decades concerning religious affiliation, practice and thought, invite us to explore some distinctions between spiritual and religious, or to think through how we will use these words. Practically speaking, I encounter assumed distinctions in my conversations regularly. I encounter it with my clients in my psychotherapy practice, and as does Tacey, with university people, both students and staff alike. I meet many people who no longer involve themselves with churches, but who continue to be interested in the religious stories of the Christian tradition, and the activities of their religious heritage, including prayer and meditation. It happened again just two weeks ago during an unplanned encounter with a new student at a university. He doesn't see himself as religious any longer, but deeply spiritual. I find this a common distinction. Ann Tormey in her doctoral dissertation quotes "Geneva," one of the women she interviewed in her PhD research that looked at the role of women in the Catholic Church as revealed in the beatification ceremony for Blessed Mary MacKillop. Geneva says: "I don't think people are on about commitment to an institutional Church in this day and age, but they are certainly on about a religious experience, going off on all sorts of off-shoots at the moment."[2] She further refers to the work of Sandra Schneiders who asserts that there is an experience of disjunction between lived faith experience and the articulation of a religious tradition. Schneiders states that the renewal of institutional Christianity will only come through the appropriation of a new Christian identity which will emerge out of the dialogue with post-modern culture. Though Geneva still refers to religious experience in her remarks, in the minds of many people "spiritual" and "religious" have now been separated, but how we distinguish between the two is unclear.

Second, as I have indicated, I agree with Jones that all people have some sort of spirituality. As Tacey says, it is a reverential attitude toward a larger sense of life. In Jones' framework, to say that all people have a spirituality, but not all practice religion, is to imply that spirituality is the larger framework, in which the practice of religion is contained. Something similar is implied by the late Rix Weaver, a Jungian analyst here in Perth, who speaks in her work, *The Old Wise Woman*, about "inner experiences out of which religions emanate."[3] From this perspective, religious experience and religions are contained in a larger reality of inner, or spiritual, experience.

Third, while the alignment of "religious" with an affiliation with a religious tradition, and the alignment of "spiritual" with a broader, or open, framework seems to be simple enough, it seems inadequate to our experience. Jung raises another important dimension of this issue. He separates the notion of religion from creed.[4] He was, at best, impatient with creedal religion that almost seemed to ignore the experience of God that for Jung was the central core of the religious experience. For Jung, then, religious experience may have little to do with religious tradition. Wallace Clift, in his work, *Jung and Christianity*, says simply, "Certainly religion is more than what goes on in churches, synagogues, and temples."[5]

Fourth, a phrase that is close to Tacey's "reverential attitude" is "religious attitude." This notion expands the issue yet further. In almost every instance "religious attitude" is used to describe an attitude in people who do not affiliate with organised religion. It also parallels closely what I have termed "spiritual" above. It is Jung's intent to affirm that there is a way of being religious without being involved in creedal affiliation or organised religion. Anthony Storr comments that Jung described the individuation process in terms of religion because the new attitude that emerged from the process had something in common with a religious attitude. The common link was the acknowledgment of a dependence upon something other than "I". Storr indicates that, for Jung, it didn't matter whether this other was located outside the psyche as God or inside the psyche as the "Self." What mattered was the attitude itself.[6] In his study of guru personalities, Storr states that a main thrust of the teaching of Bhagwan Shree Rajneesh was a "religionless religiousness." Storr observes that this attitude is consonant with Jung's point of view. The phrase carries the same intent as that of "religious attitude."[7]

Joan Chodorow[8] states that Jung's own religious attitude was shattered in his early childhood, when he associated the Lord Jesus with death. She claims that he spent his entire life re-creating what he had lost as he worked to develop ways to approach the psyche with a religious attitude. The implication in both Storr and Chodorow is that Jung's entire system is a religious undertaking. Robert Johnson parallels Chodorow's and Storr's assertion in his memoir as he tells of learning from Jung how to live with a religious attitude.[9] Johnson claims clearly that Jung's psychological term "individuation" is the equivalent of having a religious attitude towards one's life. The religious attitude/individuation process for Johnson involves listening to your interior intelligence, taking it seriously and being faithful to it. Johnson states that it includes "discovering the uniqueness of yourself, finding out who you are not and finding out who you are ... it is ... your particular relationship to everything else."[10] Johnson goes on to note that this attitude he learned from Jung subsequently opened up the depths of the symbolic systems of the world's religions. This included Christianity, which for Jung had become empty.

William James' work, *The Varieties of Religious Experience* is still a significant benchmark in the field. In it James identifies two elements that are fundamental in the religious attitude of the soul.¹¹ His notions parallel Jung's ideas. The first element is a belief in an unseen order, and the second is the understanding that our own supreme good lies in harmoniously adjusting ourselves to this unseen order. It is possible to carry this alignment further to the notion of service to the larger, unseen order, a task that is central to Christian practice.

If we work with Jung's notion of the religious attitude, then we may affirm that people are religious, and have authentic religious experiences, Christian or otherwise, even if they no longer participate in creedal, organised forms of religion. It is not appropriate then to separate spiritual and religious as if they were divided according to active participation in a religious tradition.

Yet another consideration throughout William James' work is the recognition that some spiritual experiences are not seen as religious. In his first lecture James observes: "Among the visions and messages some have always been too patently silly, among the trances and convulsive seizures some have been too fruitless for conduct and character, to pass themselves off as significant, still less as divine."¹² Later on James affirms that the process of unification of the divided self in the individual can come about over time as a psychological process with or without a religious frame of reference.¹³ Further he observes the same to be true of the spiritual process of conversion; it can be experienced as a psychological process in a non-religious frame.¹⁴

From these reflections we can identify several possible categories of experience. First, there are experiences, as James asserts above, that are psychological or spiritual that would not be considered religious by many. Second, there are experiences that are spiritual, but which would not be considered religious by those whose experiences they are. Third, there are experiences that would be deemed to be religious by those who have them. Fourth, there are experiences that might best be labelled spiritual-religious as Kelsey suggests. And just to keep us on our toes, I have found myself recently speaking of some experiences as "psycho-religious," in an attempt to honour the overlap that I perceive. While this exercise may seem tedious, it does make it clear that we use the terms in a variety of ways that are indistinct. Perhaps it also makes it clear that we are in the realm of experiences that cannot be categorised and defined into simple, tidy systems.

While I draw no tidy conclusions in this circumambulation, some things are clearer to me because of my study. These become important in reflecting on the place in psychotherapy of the spiritual or the religious. First, I affirm again that all people have a spiritual framework of some sort. The fundamental function of spirituality is to help us feel connected to our own lives however we understand and experience them and in the larger context of our shared lives with others. Second, I agree with Jung and Clift that it is possible to be religious without subscribing to creeds or dogmas, and without affiliating with a church in a particular Christian tradition. This raises questions about the place of community in one's personal spiritual-religious experience or framework, but that issue is beyond the scope of what we are addressing this evening. Third, I affirm that the development of what we have termed here a "reverential attitude", or "religious attitude" is essential to our sense of meaning and wellbeing. If spirituality has to do with the psychotherapeutic experience, then it may also have to do with the religious experience, the religious attitude and religion. At the present, I am inclined to fall back on to Kelsey's position and accept that the words spiritual and religious are linked deeply. To hyphenate them from time to time might well honour more fully the vast and overlapping territory that they are meant to describe. I also am comfortable with my own recent term of "psycho-religious" which also attempts to honour the overlap. I intend now to look at the practice of spiritual direction in the Christian tradition.

Spiritual Direction

As I have indicated, my involvement with the ministry of spiritual direction began in the late 70s when I was working with Alan Jones. Our regional training program consisted of readings from various texts, and a process of case study reflection, as well as an expectation that any person seeking to undertake such a ministry would also be receiving spiritual direction.

In the 70s and 80s this experience enjoyed a renaissance in Christian circles. It is found in the ongoing spirituality of the Roman Catholic tradition, but now is widespread in other Christian communities as well. While spiritual direction in some instances is fostered in a group setting, the dominant style of the experience is in a one-to-one encounter.

Spiritual direction in the Christian tradition is very simply a process of being concerned about an individual's relationship with God. Because of the pluralism that is in fact Christianity, there seem to be endless variations on the theme. Some prefer to refer to the practice as spiritual guidance, because the term "direction" implies power issues, or raises the fears of speaking for God. Others embrace that sense of authority and are comfortable with the responsibility of directing other souls toward God. Margaret Guenther, an Anglican priest, refers to the work as holy listening and sees the director's role as governed by the image of the midwife. Guenther's insight reminds me that, as in so many other quarters these days, women are offering the most refreshing insights into age-old theological notions and spiritual-religious practices. Some authors are utterly open-ended about the agenda for the experience, while others work from a more formatted point of view with a set agenda and sense of progress in the spiritual life. Some see it as formation within the revealed tradition, yet another colleague of mine once referred to it as a ministry of subversion in that it inevitably took the directee beyond the boundaries of conventional religious thought. Some enfold the experience of confession into the spiritual direction experience, while others would hold them separate. Another distinction within the ranks concerns the director. Some would restrict the practice to clergy only, while others insist that it is appropriate for laypersons to function as directors as well. The variations go on and on. What all would agree, and here I am assuming, is that spiritual direction has to do with one's spirituality, one's spiritual-religious experience, and one's religious attitude.

The primary focus in the spiritual direction encounter is not on the two who meet but on the relationship between the directee and God. The director, in a sense, is there to reflect on, or witness to, the movement in the primary relationship. The director is like the midwife as Guenther observes. Spiritual direction is consciously and intentionally a triangular relationship.

The process of spiritual direction is largely summed up in the word discernment. Discernment is based on the Biblical Greek word *"diakrisis,"* and refers to having right judgement. In my work as an educator in the field of spiritual direction training, I developed a three-fold way of considering discernment. What we are interested to discern is the presence, activity and will of God. Three questions bring these into focus. As we listen in the spiritual direction session we ask:

Where is the God?
What is the God doing?
What does the God want?

The first has to do with identifying God somewhere in our experiences, the second has to do with reflecting on how God is acting in our lives, and the third has to do with deciding what path of action best aligns with the will of God as we know it thus far in life and from the tradition.

This brings us to a primary consideration in spiritual direction that we have yet to address. We recognise that God is central to the process, and we can see that we are keen to discern God's presence, activity and will, but which God? It is the experience of working in spiritual direction that taught me quite clearly that people have different operative images of God, and some are not helpful. The Judeo-Christian traditions combined present us with a myriad of images for the divine life. Coupled with people's own experiences these quickly expand to countless variations. Because I consider this very important, I want to share a few stories to illustrate the issue.

About sixteen years ago, while still in the USA, a friend called and asked to see me as soon as possible. He was in considerable distress, so I invited him to come to talk with me while I washed the dinner dishes that evening. He told me that he had recently been subject to some involuntary urges that had left him almost shattered because they were the same as he had experienced about sixteen years earlier. These original experiences had led him into Jungian analysis over the intervening sixteen years with three well-known analysts. Yet here he was with the same urges or symptoms. He was devastated and concluded his remarks by saying that he did not want to do this for another sixteen years. I found myself angry with God that such a sincere and good man had to suffer like this, and there seemed no way out. Not knowing what else to say, I told him of my anger, and he made a dismissive noise about God. That opened the door, and for two years we took a journey outside the boundaries of the conventional tradition while he reconstructed a God image that was life-giving and very, very funny, and which led to a more open world view and provided a more positive psychic place for him in which to live. To put it another way, his unconscious God image was killing him. It was, by the way, through the process of active imagination that new images and possibilities emerged. I add that this man was a priest, and this made the point clearly that one can't assume that Christians have life giving images of the divine energy. I would go as far as to say that no amount of counselling, spiritual direction or psychotherapy could have opened him to healing and transformation, because of the death dealing cosmic imagery that dominated his soul. In his cosmos there was no hope. It does matter what we believe.

Another man, also a priest, once listed primary images of God in a group exercise. His first word was "judge," which explained to me the furrowed mark between his eyebrows. What is possible here? A woman worked over two years in direction on the issue of staying with or leaving her marriage. At the end of the process, in response to my question about the place of God in her struggle, she named God simply as "Presence," one who sustained her and carried her through the reflective times. Yet another woman, whose life situation many would have envied, including the rich husband, the good marriage, and interesting job, felt that life with God was more like a prison sentence than anything else. Which God? In terms of spirituality, the issue is critical. It is possible for people to labour under images, often unconscious, that are neither life giving nor that enable change. The images themselves may be part of the oppression and wounding of the soul.

While this issue of the God image seems the domain of spiritual direction, it seems to me that it is worthy of consideration in any one-to-one work, including psychotherapy. If, as I propose, it is true that these images construct a worldview that, if unquestioned, may inhibit or prevent the possibilities of transformation, then they need to be brought into the light of conscious reflection for careful consideration. I would suggest that there is a challenge here for practitioners to be able to explore the belief systems of clients in a constructive manner as part of the psychotherapeutic process. Having now considered the experience of spiritual direction, including the process of discernment and the importance of the God images, I now want to draw some distinctions between spiritual direction and psychotherapy.

Spiritual Direction and Psychotherapy: Some Distinctions

I admit at the outset that I find this section most difficult, because of my personal perspective. I believe that there are many similarities between spiritual direction and psychotherapy. In terms of distinctions, the first involves the starting place of the processes. A friend observed years ago that often people begin spiritual direction with a desire to grow and in the process encounter a crisis, while in psychotherapy people often begin in crisis and stay to grow. The experiences seem, by and large, to start at different places.

Second, one spiritual director notes that people in spiritual direction must have a sense of personal freedom to undertake the journey, but people in psychotherapy often have little sense of personal freedom at the outset of their therapy. There is often a different capacity for freedom and, therefore, for action at the outset.

Third, I would suggest that there is a difference concerning the focus of attention between the two experiences. In the psychotherapeutic encounter the attention is on the client and the issues that are presented. This focus then expands to include the client-therapist relationship, the therapeutic alliance. It is a direct two-way relationship. In the spiritual direction encounter the focus is on God as the ground of experience for the client. The primary focus is the God relationship for the directee. Whatever transpires in the spiritual direction setting, there is always the sense of a third party being present. In direction, we understand ourselves in the context of the God-human relationship. God is the context, God is the reference point, God is the journey, and God is the journey's end. Because of the focus on the divine life in the spiritual direction experience, I would also suggest that the experience of transference is less likely to occur between the director and directee.

Fourth, the idea of focus leads us to reflect on the context and framework of psychotherapy and spiritual direction. The framework of spiritual direction is cosmic in scope. It deals explicitly with metaphysical concerns. Within this point of view, we might go so far as to assert that the encounter between God, the directee and the director is an act of worship. It may involve times of silence and prayer, even the laying on of hands for healing and the ritual of confession. The directee places her or his own story in the story of a People, and this story contributes to one's own identity.

The psychotherapeutic encounter also takes place within a framework and context. It may seem less clear because there may be a greater difference between the worldviews of the therapist and the client at the outset. The therapist invites the client into a setting that is held in a perspective on the nature of the psychotherapeutic encounter. The therapist presents her or himself and guides the work in the context of a belief system about humanity and the work itself. The client enters the encounter bringing his or her framework. How the two frameworks and contexts interact and how the worldviews of both will shift is revealed only over time. In our initial exchanges with clients, we may reveal something of the framework in which we live and into which we welcome people. On the other hand, there are some instances when we withhold deliberately our points of view in the interests of providing a more neutral and open setting in which the client may examine his or her own material more freely. But this withholding, too, is part of the belief that informs our work.

In addition to these, I note several simple points of difference between spiritual direction and psychotherapy. In many instances spiritual direction is offered at no charge. Rarely is therapy offered at no charge. Spiritual direction is less intense in terms of the frequency of meetings. The usual pace of the work is monthly, sometimes fortnightly. Therapy sessions, as we know usually are more frequent. Spiritual direction seems like a more mutual experience, with relaxed attitudes about self-disclosure on the part of the director. By contrast, many therapists keep strict boundaries around their personal lives. I would suggest that interactions with directees apart from sessions is far more common than encounters between client and therapist apart from sessions. While both spiritual direction and psychotherapy overlap greatly in dealing with the soul, I intuit that they do so differently, and I hope that these distinctions offer a bit of clarity as to how this is so.

A Healthy Spirituality

Finally, I want to highlight briefly some characteristics of a healthy spirituality. Again, my perspective is my version of a Christian point of view. In my reflections over many years on spirituality, I have concluded that there are four essential characteristics that mark a healthy spirituality in our time. A healthy spirituality is inclusive, diverse, experiential, and simple.

1) It is inclusive in that it gathers in all the different aspects of who we are and makes of them a whole. The overall movement of the spiritual life is one of integration and inclusiveness. A healthy spirituality does not demand the denial or dismissal of troublesome parts of who we are. It pulls together and coheres around a central reality, the divine life. Transformation is through engagement, reconciliation, making peace, building bridges, being decisive and making room for the others within. An old, wise woman once said in this regard, "Include no one out."

2) A healthy spirituality is also one that is diverse. It is a perspective that makes room for differences and sees differences as natural and desirable. This includes differences not only among us who are indeed very different, but also differences within us. This extends to include our ambivalent points of view, and our different perspectives at different times of life. In this spiritual picture, cloning is not a virtue. Alan Jones asserts that we are each "a unique and unrepeatable event."

   Diversity extends also to community. From my perspective it is important to affirm that, while we each may experience a sense of wholeness within ourselves, human life is not whole in isolation from others. Human communities in many diverse forms express a wholeness that enriches and deepens the human experience for us as individuals.

3) A healthy spirituality is grounded in our personal experience. While it is a sign of wisdom and humility to be respectful of the experiences of our forebears, is it not helpful to base our worldview solely on the experiences of others. In a sense each person must claim as our own the traditions and insights of the People who have gone before us. It is essential, therefore, to question and to critique what others have experienced. Some things we may revere, and others we may set aside. It is essential to develop self-reflective skills that allow us to examine and assess our own experience with care.

4) A healthy spirituality also leads to simplicity. This elusive quality represents the process of distilling out of the ambiguity and complexity of life an essential and simple truth or truths by which to live our days. Personally, at present I am not sure this can happen for most young people. Simplicity seems to come slowly with age. When I was twenty-six, I heard a retired bishop who was close to one hundred years old speak at a public gathering. His words were few, but well chosen, and he spoke as if life was very simple. How could it be, I wondered? Now at fifty-seven I am beginning to understand a little. A healthy spirituality rests increasingly on a bedrock foundation of simple truths that are distilled out from our experiences over the years. I also believe that, in some way the emergence of simplicity also may lead to simplification in one's life.

Inclusive, diverse, experiential, simple, these four are the essential characteristics of a healthy spirituality. The growing realisation of these in our lives can cultivate three qualities within us. First, we develop a positive sense of self regard, or self-love. Second, we find within ourselves the strength to cope with whatever life deals out, as life tends to do. Third, we identify an appropriate place for ourselves in the world; we find our "place" both within the human family and in the larger creation. Each of these invites much reflection.

Concluding thoughts

We come to the end of this exercise, and I have two concluding points to offer. First, from my perspective, spirituality is integral to psychotherapy. I see psychotherapy as a sacred process, a psycho-religious process that includes addressing matters of soul. Perhaps then, to respond to the task of this evening a little differently, the concern is not for spirituality and psychotherapy, but for the spirituality that is contained within any experience of psychotherapy. The concern is for the spirituality *in* psychotherapy. That leads me to the second point. The character of spirituality in a psychotherapeutic encounter largely begins with the therapist. In time the spiritualities of the therapist and client will interact and, ideally, transform both. The challenge of our reflection is to ask ourselves about our own frameworks and perspectives on spirituality. What is my personal sense of spirituality, what is it I believe and what is it I do in terms of connections? How do I discover and make connections with Other – God – the divine energy, with myself, with others and with the world? How does this contribute to my healing and transformation and to my wellbeing? I am quite convinced that spiritualities operate in any therapeutic encounter, and that if I am conscious and intentional about it, the effect of it is more beneficial.

I conclude with a brief story out of my own experience that has been formative. When I was about eighteen, I was discussing the notion of healing with my priest, Morton Kelsey, whom I have already mentioned. I don't now remember the conversation, but I do remember its ending. After we had knocked around a few ideas, Kelsey concluded, "It all depends on your point of view." I've found this one-liner of significant assistance over the years. In terms of the spirituality in psychotherapy, my own point of view is central. I do carry my spirituality into every encounter I have in my study. It acts as a beginning framework and is often a resource for tried and tested insights and practices that may contribute to a way forward for another. It certainly shapes the way in which I approach the souls of others. Therefore, my point of view matters greatly. To carry this consciously, to name it within myself, to understand its presence and significance, certainly provides a safer and more transformative environment for the healing of others.

Endnotes

1. The quotes here are from the interview conversations I had with Morton Kelsey in January 1998, in San Diego California, as part of my PhD research.
2. Tormey, Ann. *The Beatification of Mary MacKillop*. p. 213.
3. Weaver, Rix. *The Old Wise Woman:* p. 151.
4. Jung, Carl. G. *The Collected Works of C. G. Jung*. Vol. 18. para. 1637.
5. Clift, Wallace. *Jung and Christianity*. p. 65.
6. Storr, Anthony. 1972. *The Dynamics of Creation*. pp. 286–87.
7. Storr, Anthony. 1996. *Feet of Clay*. p. 51.

8. Chodorow, Joan. *Jung on Active Imagination.* p. 2.
9. Johnson, Robert. *Balancing Heaven and Earth.* p. 171.
10. Ibid.
11. James, William. *The Varieties of Religious Experience.* p. 53.
12. Ibid. p. 20.
13. Ibid. p. 175.
14. Ibid. p. 189.

References

Chodorow, Joan. 1997. Introduction. In: *Jung on Active Imagination.* Princeton: Princeton University Press.

Clift, Wallace. 1982. *Jung and Christianity: The Challenge of Reconciliation.* Melbourne: Collins Dove.

James, William. 1902/1985. *The Varieties of Religious Experience: A Study in Human Nature.* New York: Penguin Books Penguin Classics.

Johnson, Robert, with Jerry. R. Ruhl. 1998. *Balancing Heaven and Earth. A Memoir.* New York: HarperSanFrancisco.

Jung, Carl. G. 1958/1980. Jung and Religious Belief. In: *The Collected Works of C. G. Jung.* (R. F. C. Hull, Trans.) Vol. 18. Princeton: Princeton University Press.

Storr, Anthony. 1972. *The Dynamics of Creation.* London: Penguin Books.

Storr, Anthony. 1996. *Feet of Clay: A Study of Gurus.* London: HarperCollins*Publishers.*

Tormey, Ann. 1998. *The Beatification of Mary MacKillop: What it Reveals of the Experience of Women in the Contemporary Catholic Church.* Unpublished Doctoral Dissertation, Edith Cowan University, Perth, Western Australia.

Weaver, Rix. 1973. *The Old Wise Woman: A Study in Active Imagination*. New York: G. p. Putnam Sons for the C. G. Jung Foundation of Analytical Psychology.

My Experience of Self

I presented this talk at a conference entitled "Spirituality and the Marketplace," in Fremantle, Western Australia on 20 February 2004. Several of us speakers were asked to address briefly our experience of the notion of the self. I present this here with a single sentence edit.

At first, I was grateful to be asked to offer my personal reflections on the notion of "self" at this gathering. However, when I began to consider my task sitting in front of the computer, my gratitude slipped quickly to frustration. Fortunately, all that gave way to amusement, as I remembered the observation of a colleague made years ago. He once remarked that if it fits on a bumper sticker, it's probably a lie. Recognising, then, that I can't make this reflection on "self" simple and tidy, I have decided to ramble around four basic points that have characterised my experience of the notion of self across the course of my years.

Aware

I am a Christian from my early days, and now an Anglican priest, a fringe dweller in my community. "Churchianity" worries me, yet the Christ story still speaks deeply to me. In my home parish in California, great emphasis was placed on self-awareness. The rector himself had spent a sabbatical in Zurich studying at the Jung Institute, and Carl Jung's psychology deeply influenced his understanding of the Christ story. I began my therapeutic work at fifteen and spiritual direction at sixteen with two men who worked in the Christian-Jungian model, and it has marked my life. I have continued from that time forward to take my dreams seriously as a primary resource for self-understanding, guidance and meaning for my life.

In Jung's psychology as I understand it, the highest ethic and the overall goal is self-consciousness, self-awareness. Even though it would fit on a bumper sticker, the Socratic assertion "know thyself" was an important statement, and a challenge for my life. I concluded early on that most of the destructive things we do spring from, or are fuelled by, a lack of self-awareness. This is certainly true of me.

In the early years I was confused about the Christian virtue of humility in reference to self-awareness. What I saw being offered as examples of humility looked too much like low self-esteem and were not at all attractive. It was the writings of Teresa of Avila that shifted this for me and helped me realise that humility is an important aspect of self-awareness. I draw from her work the insight that humility is the ability to practice an honest self-assessment, to know our strengths and weaknesses and to honour both. Teresa held self-awareness to be the entry-level concern for her form of a spiritual life.

My Experience of Self

From 1980 to 1985, in the USA, I was helping train spiritual directors as part of a national program. I worked with Alan Jones, who is now the Dean of Grace Cathedral in San Francisco. Alan once described each of us as a "unique and unrepeatable event." In terms of self-awareness, I have found this an important insight. There is no one quite like me, for which, by the way, my mother will give eternal thanks. With this understanding comes, for me, a sense of excitement, as well as the challenge to stand alone at times amid the human enterprise. Even as we are in the midst, we each, in some sense, undertake this journey of self in a way that no one has before.

Strong

From self-awareness I want to move to the notion of a strong sense of self. The writer of the Biblical Book of Luke attributes these words to Jesus of Nazareth in chapter 9:23-24: "If any want to become my followers, let them deny themselves and take up their cross daily and follow me. For those who want to save their life will lose it, and those who lose their life for my sake will find it."

I remember taking my confusion over this passage to my priest when I was a teenager. He encouraged me to realise that I can only give up what I first possess, therefore it is critical to develop a strong sense of self in order to then align oneself with a larger reality. For me, that insight supported developing a strong sense of self. A well-known story from the sacred texts tells of the encounter between God and Moses at the burning bush in the wilderness. It is at this meeting that Moses is given his first duties statement. The exchange and the task given to Moses enhance the importance of a strong sense of self. In the encounter God revealed the divine life as "I am who I am." I conclude that this is a goal for each of us: to know, to claim, and then to be, who I am.

The development of a strong sense of self, and here I mean ego consciousness, has included learning how to set boundaries, which popular religious piety in my tradition often does not honour. At times we appear to honour more those who serve 'til they drop. I have had to learn to say "no," and among my learning experiences was a serious, six-month depression, twenty-five years ago, brought on by my misguided desire to serve and please. I had betrayed myself and I paid a high price.

Context

In recent years I have come to conclude that a strong sense of self involves moving from being a referential person to a self-referential person, who affirms the truth for my life primarily from within. Much of the work in my present psychotherapy practice involves assisting people in transferring the locus of authority from outside somewhere, to inside, to the self within. It does seem that most of us are socialised not to listen respectfully to, or to trust, the voice of our own souls.

Yet self-awareness and a strong sense of being guided by our truth from within, must be balanced by a sense of self in context. John Donne's insight, that no one is an island, even though the words might fit on a bumper sticker, still carries significant truth. The challenge of Jesus in the passage quoted earlier is to place this self that we both discover and develop, at the service of something larger than ourselves. William James, in his classic lectures on religious experience, describes this as the fundamental identifying characteristic of a religious attitude. We acknowledge that there is some life force, energy, larger than ourselves and realise that it is in our best interests to align ourselves with this reality. This is the point my priest made to me as a teenager. We develop a strong sense of self; we move from being referential to self-referential and then work to align ourselves with a larger life. We live in reference to a larger truth.

It was very important to me while in university to read of a distinction between individualism and Jung's notion of "individuation." As I have come to understand it, "individuation" means that we each must, across the course of our lives, separate ourselves from the collective thinking and values of our tribe or clan, and discover the uniqueness of who we are. In the course of this ongoing experience, we also become aware of how much we are like others, and how ordinary we are. This sense of self leads us back to our people to whom we contribute from our uniqueness, and with whom we share our common, ordinary lives. We come full circle to understand ourselves as both a unique and ordinary person in the context of a people. This movement out from our tribe or group and our return with a new sense of self is a journey of heroic magnitude. For me, it represents an essential aspect of a mature self. To say it another way, what I do for myself, I do not do for me alone. I have come to realise that I am not, in any significant way, an endpoint in my own life. The dance between self and other never ends throughout our lives. While my self-discovery and self-development are essential to my human experience, my relationships are also central, core, critical to what I come to understand and experience of my self. To say it another way, there are times when it is you who save me from myself.

Mystery

The notions of self-awareness, a strong sense of self, and self in context must finally be joined by the sense of mystery. There is a paradox here, and someone once remarked that paradox is a sure sign of truth in human experience. In my youth I was driven by the virtue of self-consciousness, self-awareness. Imagine then, me coming up against a schematic presentation at a conference years ago, which asserted that, to some degree I do not know, and will never, know myself. I will always be a bit of mystery to myself. In 1975, at a conference on Mystery, I heard the late Dr. Margaret Mead make this same assertion about God. God is always more than we will ever know. I, who valued consciousness as the highest virtue, found these encounters with mystery somewhat disorienting, even frightening. The years have eased the fright and brought instead relief. For all that I understand of myself, all that I have discovered and all that I have worked to develop, I still engage myself as a bit of a mystery. Most often these days there is some delight in this, but now and then there is a twinge of disquiet.

Self: aware, strong, in context and shrouded in mystery. In the Prologue to his memoirs, *Memories, Dreams, Reflections*, Jung reminds us that "At bottom we never know how it has all come about." Thank you.

Masculine Spirituality

I was invited to offer this reflection as a sermon at morning worship at the Mt. Hawthorn Community Church in Western Australia in November 2006. It was based on a much longer morning lecture presentation I made at the Dayspring Centre for Spirituality in February 2005. I have edited the 2006 text here to suit a more general audience. The focus of my concerns sixteen years ago may seem dated in one way, yet they still raise important issues in our ongoing conversations about the nature of the masculine energy and of spirituality.

I begin this morning by expressing my thanks to Tyson Menck for initiating this opportunity. As I have anticipated being here today, I haven't always been so thankful or excited, as the task seems daunting, but as we gather, I am content to be here and to have the opportunity to share some thoughts with you. At the outset I want to change the focus of the topic. To address masculine spirituality, I intend to present four challenges that I have identified in my personal inner work and in my work with men over the years.

There are two initial matters to address briefly as we begin. First, the spectrum of masculine spirituality is such that it is more appropriate to talk about masculinities and spiritualities. There is no one single or simple way to express the nature of the masculine in our lives, and the variation of spiritualities is endless. Two writers who have contributed to this conversation are Eugene Monick in his book, *Phallos: Sacred Image of the Masculine*, and Jean Shinoda Bolen in her book, *Gods in Everyman*. These are very helpful resources.

Second, I want to be clear in this church setting that my personal framework is strongly and decidedly Christ centred, though not necessarily in a traditional way. My own spiritual life and practices are deeply influenced by the work of Carl Jung and my language reflects this. I am reflecting here on matters of spirituality for men who are seeking to walk in the Christ way, but I am just as concerned in speak in such a way that men of other faith traditions or none may also find the matters raised here to be of interest to them. Let's now take a tour of these four challenges.

First, in considering spiritualities and masculinities, we men must separate masculinity from patriarchy. I have come to believe that this is a critical step to take with conscious intention. However we have used the term "patriarchy" in times past, today it is commonly used to describe a social reality or structure that results when relational and corporate structures are designed by men drawing on a particular aspect of the masculine energy. This design takes for granted male superiority and male privilege and is preferential to the male at every turn. This design, I suggest, is grounded in the notion of God as male, which springs from the very heart of popular, traditional Christian thought. In its practical expression in my experience, this design has preferred white, heterosexual males, in western culture quite exclusively. The dominance of this model can hardly be ignored. It pervades the design of our western social structures and relationships at every level. In terms of our Christian religious tradition, the patriarchal design has influenced deeply the mainline traditional church structures we have established, our ways of theologising about God and humanity, and the perspective from which our sacred texts are interpreted.

As a result of patriarchal dominance, women, and many men who are identified as part of any racial, ethnic, or psycho-sexual minority group, have lived with a second-class status at best. They have been oppressed, treated unjustly, abused, belittled, devalued, dehumanised, and even killed. For most of us, many women and large numbers of men, "patriarchy" describes the current villain in the piece. The design it represents is the subject of much justified criticism and has been targeted appropriately for radical change.

Eugene Monick asserts that the fusion of masculinity with patriarchy is an untenable situation for males in terms of our psycho-spiritual health and wellbeing. As he states simply in his work, "Unless masculinity is differentiated from patriarchy, both will go down the drain together."[1]

Fortunately, we can see now that the spectrum of masculinities is broader than we have ever imagined. Some years ago, a man who came to see me for counseling, asked simply, "Between the wimp and rambo, what is there?" The ground-breaking works of Monick and Bolen assist us in realising that there are many, even countless options between the wimp and rambo.

We can now affirm that what we name as "patriarchy" is but a very narrow sliver out of the amazing spectrum of masculinities. It is critical for us to affirm this, for unless we men can realise that we have countless options between the wimp and rambo, we risk getting stuck in cartoon like images of masculinity, and flounder in frustration, fear, and guilt in the search for life-giving spiritualities that will work for us. So, to begin, we men must do the work of dismantling patriarchy and undertake to explore the wonderful variations of masculinities.

Second, in the search for life giving masculinities and spiritualities, we men must affirm women in their distinct and separate identities and affirm as well the integrity of the feminine. We are challenged to engage the feminine with serious intent, respect, and humility. From my point of view, both women and the feminine are downgraded and degraded by traditional patriarchal attitudes. Men, I believe, must affirm the equality of women to themselves, and in this be careful not to use the "equal but different" approach to escape confrontation with the simple reality of equality, and the profound value and importance of the feminine, and of women. As well, men must affirm the integrity of the feminine energy as equal in importance to the masculine. This is true of the feminine in God, in women, and of the feminine in us men. It has long been my conviction that until we reframe our imagined concepts of creation and affirm the mutual presence of the feminine and masculine in the divine imagery from the very moment of creation, we will not be able to effect spiritual, psychological, and social structures that are truly equal.

This issue of the feminine within us is, for me, critical, for I have come to believe that for men "she" is the bridge to our own unconscious depths. "She" is the one who makes it possible for a man to develop a spirituality of depth, richness, and vitality. Without her we may well only harden into some inflexible and petrified cartoon of some aspect of the masculine, and then be swamped from time to time by unintegrated emotions of life that will cause us to wallow in infantile sentimentality. With the assistance of the feminine our hearts are broken open to astonishing tenderness, profound compassion, and suffering love – all things Godly. With her we have the chance in this life of actually becoming human, and maybe even Christian. To say it more simply if we men want to be truly manly, we must engage this mysterious feminine within our own souls and with the women around us. It is she who will enable a soulful depth to our experience of being Man.

In the present conversation around masculinities and spiritualities, there are some who would dismiss this imagery of masculine and feminine altogether or to see them simply as social constructions. I respond differently. Being influenced deeply by Carl Jung's psychology, and the importance of archetypal images, I find it more enriching and challenging to wrestle with the images of masculine and feminine as first archetypal energies, then cultural and personal expressions. I sense it as deeply meaningful to speak of masculine and feminine as sacred, trans-cultural, primordial energies, the union of which is the divine intent at all levels. Something of the God is in all this, and it carries an ethical imperative for me. This imperative includes finding ways to speak of gender equality, to honour the union of the two energies in each male and female, and to find ways to speak of God newly, so that both masculine and feminine are seen as springing from the heart, the very centre of the divine life.

Third, in seeking to cultivate life-giving spiritualities and masculinities, I believe men must affirm the integrity, even the rights of the creation, of which we males are only a part. The global environmental crises that face the human family have been brought upon us largely by a degradation of nature and the created order largely at the hands of the traditional patriarchal values of western capitalist, consumer cultures. It seems to me that these values have been thoughtlessly supported in the western world by the Christian movement, which, historically, has lost sight of its own values for the creation of which we were meant to be stewards. Aside from Saint Francis in history and the creation spirituality movement of recent times, we haven't done well in honouring the creation, though there is ample biblical material available on which to build a more sensitive understanding, especially in the Psalms. While the historical reasons for this may be very complex, certainly part of the problem has been our traditional and unfortunate interpretation of Genesis 3. In the famous story misnamed "The Fall," neither women nor creation have fared well due to our interpretation and use of the story. I have also come across an attitude on the part of some western Christians who see the degradation of the environment and the tragic wars in which we seem to engage endlessly, as positive signs of the end times. With all this degradation and violence going on, so the reasoning goes, surely the end is coming when the faithful will be taken up into heaven and the rest of us destroyed. The line of thought seems to align all this tragedy with the will of God, which the faithful should not oppose, but therefore must stand back and let it all unfold as it is. I have read some sources that connect such thinking specifically to the American Religious Right, which includes a disturbing number of American national legislators. I find such thinking ungodly at best; it is to be disavowed at every opportunity.

I invite us to consider seriously again our original roles as stewards of this wondrous creation, and to renew our efforts to work for its health and wellbeing. I am pleased to note that the crisis of global warming seems now to be receiving more attention among our national and state leaders, and creation minded citizens' groups. I am finding it more and more to be important to re-train my thinking, and to consider in every possible instance my impact on my/our natural environment. The planet earth is my/our home, and Saint Francis wasn't off with the fairies when he named aspects of the creation as siblings and family members. One task of a mature and wholesome spirituality in Christ is to place ourselves directly in the family of creation and to live more responsibly with our family members.

Fourth, in our search into the realms of spiritualities and masculinities, we men must reconsider our relationship with our own bodies. In 1984 I ended up in the hospital in California with chest pains and pains down my left arm. It had been a hellish time in my work, and I was losing my grip. I soldiered on with these symptoms for several days before admitting to them, and shortly after I owned up, my wife and I were at the hospital. I was checked out over several days, and finally after a treadmill test the cardiologist assured me that I had not had a heart attack but a stress reaction. He then asked a bit about my present life. I told him and he listened quite patiently. He concluded by telling me to go on home, and take it easy for a few more days, and allowed as how I could proceed with my plans to come here to Australia to offer my workshops and lectures. I was in good health, he told me, and his last piece of blunt advice was to quit my job. As it happened, within the year I did just that.

For many of us men, to consider seriously our relationship with our bodies will be a first-time discovery. In spite of whatever sexual abilities men are supposed to have, and in spite of the trendy modes of exercise that leave many panting and gasping through the culture, most men are out of touch with their bodies. I found an interesting observation in an essay by Scott Russell, entitled, "Fathers, Sons, Sports", in an issue of *Harper's* magazine some years ago. He is reflecting on his own question, "Why do we play these games so avidly?" To this he gives first what he calls a Freudian answer, in which playing with balls takes on masturbatory overtones. Then he proposes a Darwinian answer which has to do with strutting male peacocks. Third he considers a biological answer that has to do with levels of testosterone, and then an economic answer that has to do with fantasies of the large pay checks of the professionals. Russell then says: "No doubt each of those explanations, like buckets put out in the rain, catch some of the truth. But none of them catches all the truth. None of them explains, for example, what moves a boy to bang a rubber ball against a wall for hours, for entire summers, as my father did in his youth, as I did in mine, as Jesse, my son, still does. That boy throwing and catching in the lee of garage or barn, dwells for a time wholly in his body, and that is reward enough. He aims a ball at a knothole, at a crack, then leaps to snag the rebound, mastering a skill, working himself into a trance. How different is his rapture from the dancing and drumming of a young brave? How different is his solitude from that of any boy seeking visions?"[2]

Russell begins his next paragraph with this provocative sentence: "The less use we have for our bodies, the more we need reminding that the body possesses its own way of knowing."[3] The rediscovery of brother body with its own way of knowing, includes learning natural and spiritual truths from our bodies, as I believe women have done for so long. The simple, startling question is: "What does my male body teach me of myself, and of the ways of God."

Monick has some challenging insights about all this. He pushes us further than any other contemporary writer I have read in proposing that the sexual energy manifest in our psyches and displayed in the arousal experiences of our bodies, is at the core a sacred energy. Therefore, in every experience of arousal there are intimations of God present, and a man is in the presence of the holy at such a time. There is a union of our spiritualities with our sexualities implied here which Kenneth Leech, in his work, *Soul Friend: A Study in Spirituality*, states more directly. Leech says, "Religion and sex are inextricably linked, and the honest facing of human sexuality is vital to spirituality. When it does not happen, spirituality becomes twisted and unbalanced."[4]

Such a linking of sexualities to our spiritualities indicates a deeply integrated and Incarnational perspective of the partnership of body and soul in this life journey and offers us the possibility that our bodies are not only our companions in the Way of Christ, but they are also at times our teachers and guides.

In exploring masculinities and spiritualities I have presented these four challenges as essential to our tasks as men. Here are the four I identify once again. 1) Men must separate masculinity from patriarchy, 2) men must affirm women in their own distinct identities and affirm the importance and integrity of the feminine as well, 3) men must affirm the integrity of the creation, our extended family, and 4) men must give serious consideration to their relationship to their own bodies, including their sexualities.

I believe that it is out of consideration of these challenges that we can cultivate appropriate practices and disciplines that will be life-giving for us as men seeking to walk in the Christ way.

There is much more to consider in these four challenges and in the areas of our masculinities and our spiritualities. I hope that my brief remarks provoke further thought and reflection and action.

Endnotes

1. Monick, Eugene. *Phallos*. p. 9.
2. Russell, Scott. "Fathers, Sons, Sports." p. 35.
3. Ibid.
4. Leech, Kenneth. *Soul Friend*. p.113.

References

Bolen, Jean Shinoda. 1989. *Gods in Everyman*. San Francisco: Harper & Row Publishers.

Leech, Kenneth. 1977. *Soul Friend: A Study in Spirituality*. London: Sheldon Press.

Monick, Eugene. 1987. *Phallos: Sacred Image of the Masculine*. Toronto: Inner City Books.

Russell, Scott. 1991. "Fathers, Sons, Sports." in *Harper's*. June 1991.

The Jonah Syndrome: Do You Get It?

The presentations on the Jonah story began as a weekend retreat for men in 2007, and soon after I offered the same material at a day-long event. I have created the following essay under this new title from those original notes augmented with current reflections. My intention is to use this great story to consider our relationship with our God, however named. Readers may find it helpful to refresh themselves to the story in the Bible before reading through this reflection.

Introduction

There are many variations on the title question. A man tells his friend a joke and the befuddled look on the face of the listener prompts the storyteller to ask, "Do you get it?" In the breakdown of a relationship, she says of him, "He just doesn't get it! In a tension filled conversation about vaccination in the recent Covid virus pandemic a woman throws up her hands in frustration over the anti-vaxxer position and exclaims, "I just don't get it!" At the end of a conversation about the stance of the government concerning climate change a man declares dismissively, "They just don't get it"! Variations can include, "We're not on the same page." "He'll never understand." "She just cannot get what I am saying." There are times and in a variety of settings when I realise, I just don't get it.

Set in the context of Jonah's relationship with his God are several important issues that are part of any spiritual framework. One core issue is the experiences of difference in countless forms and circumstances. We are challenged time and again to try to understand from our individual life box the life boxes others choose to live in, struggle in, are trapped in, hide in, or feel safe and are liberated in. Climbing out of our box and seeing life from another perspective is a serious challenge, and no more than in the larger frame of Jonah's relationship with his God.

My reflections on the story of Jonah began many years ago. As I prepared finally to create reflections for presentation on this great story, I found a website by Rebbetzin Tzipporah Heller on Jonah and the whale. I learned from her work that the story of Jonah is read every year in the synagogue on Yom Kippur. The story carries the essence of that day and its central theme, the return to God. Central themes include engaging differences, repentance, and forgiveness. Heller remarks: "It teaches us about our voyage and ourselves."[1] She asserts that Jonah's journey is one that we all make. In this sense then the story of Jonah is available to each of us as a symbolic and archetypal story about our relationship with our God, however we define our God. It is a story about us.

The story of Jonah has its roots in an historical person, a

prophet among the people. Heller tells us that Jonah lived in the first Temple period, and sources record that he was given two previous tasks, or missions. Elijah assigned Jonah his first task. He was assigned to anoint Jehu as King in the year 705BCE. His second task was to rebuke Jeroboam II, Jehu's successor. Heller tells us that this second mission failed. Jonah's third and final mission is the one we find in our Biblical story. It was assigned to him by his God. He was to declare doom on the city of Ninevah, "that great city," in Assyria. It was a task he did not want to undertake, and the biblical story begins. Whatever we make of the interrelationship of history and myth in these sacred texts and traditions about Jonah, our intention here is to use this great wisdom story to reflect on our relationship with our God.

Moving into the sacred texts of the Christian tradition, we find two references to Jonah as a sign to the people, both remarks are attributed to Jesus. The references are Matthew 12:38-42 and Luke 11:29-32. In each the text is different as is the emphasis on Jonah as a sign. In the Matthean version there is mention of the three days and nights in the belly of the great fish. The writer uses Jonah as a precursor of the death and resurrection journey of Christ. The writer of Luke has a different emphasis. Here the focus is on Jonah's prophetic role. The prophetic task is to call the Ninevites to repentance in the face of impending doom. Their repentance becomes a judgement on the present generation of Jonah's people. In these two texts Jesus declares forcefully that the people will be given no other sign. This certainly heightens the importance of Jonah as a prophet and example for the people, and Heller reminds us that it is also a story about us.

As we engage this remarkable story, I intend to focus on three images. They are the *storm*, the *belly*, and the *plant*. In the spirit of Jung, we will walk around in these images and as we do, we will see what emerges for us. My hope is that these reflections help us engage the story of Jonah as our story and open us to new depths and meanings in our relationship with our God, however named.

The Storm

Alignment

The storm is where we begin. Jonah is challenged with a mission: The Lord says: "Go at once to Nineveh, that great city, and cry out against it; for their wickedness has come up before me." (Jonah 1:2) Jonah hears the summons and he takes off in another direction entirely. He goes to Joppa to find a boat that will take him to Tarshish. He has no intention of taking up the challenge of his God. God commands and Jonah flees; such is the relationship.

As we reflect on this as our story as well, we are invited to give thought to our relationship with our God, however we imagine and name this divine life. The dynamic here is alignment. How do I align myself, my thoughts, values, principles, and my activities – my entire sense of myself – with divinity, as I understand divinity, or God? Alignment with my God; this is the fundamental challenge.

William James, in *The Varieties of Religious Experience,* defines the religious attitude as having two parts.[2] The first consists of the belief in an unseen order, and the second is to acknowledge that our supreme good lies in harmoniously aligning ourselves with it. God directs Jonah to Nineveh; Jonah heads for Joppa and Tarshish. Jonah does not align himself with God's plan.

Weyler Greene, a Jungian analyst, commented to me many years ago, that each of us at some point must undergo a Copernican revolution of the soul, that is, to realise that we are not the centre around which all else revolves. We are the centre of nothing really, but revolve around a larger life, like the earth revolves around the sun. God says, "Go at once to Nineveh;" Jonah heads for Joppa and Tarshish.

Another Jungian Analyst, Edward Edinger, in his work, *Ego and Archetype*, asserts that Jonah could not accept the challenge of God because he was still too inflated to acknowledge the authority of his God. It was only after his futile efforts to escape that he was able to acknowledge and accept the transpersonal authority of God.[3] The challenge we ponder here is to align ourselves with the purposes, the summons, of the divine life ... and Jonah is off to Joppa and Tarshish.

Alignment for me raises the issue of the "place" of the ego in a soulful spirituality. In my experience of popular contemporary spirituality, the ego often gets bad press. Once I had a rather tense conversation with a person who said with lament, "If I could only get my ego out of the way." I couldn't let that go by and suggested that a weak or undervalued ego might well lead to mental illness, and that won me no points that day. It takes a strong ego to navigate the complexities of human life and the disciplines of any spiritual tradition and practice. My understanding is that the ego functions to help us engage safely and appropriately with the world around us. The ego facilitates, discerns, makes choices, sets boundaries, and negotiates, as we move through life.

If we consider the experience of ego on a broad spectrum, we can see that, at one far end, the ego can be controlling to a tyrannical degree, much like the mad Herod in the Biblical narratives about the birth of Jesus in Matthew's story. On the other far end the ego can be so undeveloped that we have no strong sense of self or boundaries, and are overrun both from without and from within, and our mental health is in jeopardy. Mature spiritualities involve a flexible ego that is both strong in terms of our identity and sense of self, and malleable in terms of placing ourselves at the service of a larger life, in this case, divinity. It takes a strong ego to align ourselves with, to place ourselves in the service of, our God.

Resistance

Jonah receives the challenge, "Go at once to Nineveh," and his ego says, "No." He sets off for Joppa and Tarshish. Jonah resists, and this is our second theme on which to reflect. Jonah resists the summons, the will of God. It is an understandable response. To go to preach doom in an enemy camp is a bit crazy.

There are times when it seems sensible to resist the challenges of God. The writer of the Biblical book of Hebrews asserts in 10:31, that "It is a fearful thing to fall into the hands of the living God." In the Biblical book of Exodus, chapter 3, we see that Moses had a similar response to God who appeared in the burning bush. God challenged Moses to go to Egypt and lead the people out into freedom, and he came up with all sorts of excuses why he couldn't do so, until God put down the proverbial foot, so to speak, and told him to get on with it.

How is resistance a part of our stories? There are those times when the call, the summons of our God, the divine wisdom, challenges us to undertake an action or attitude that requires significant change. We are summoned to a new sense of self, to a deeper understanding of others, or to a new adventure in our journey, and we must make a response. We are challenged to step outside the box of what has been familiar and secure and to launch ourselves into an uncertain unknown.

I can see the pattern of resistance in my own story. It took me about ten years to face my alcohol addiction and to accept the challenge of sobriety. I resisted the challenge with "religious devotion," until the more attractive picture of a sober me finally won out over the former picture of the imbibing me that my controlling ego defended for several years. I also remember at age 48 being challenged to commit to setting up a private practice in my 50th year. I had plenty of lead time to prepare and grow into that new self-concept, but my ego was overwhelmed by the challenge of this new picture of me. I looked back over my shoulder for security to the way things had been and moved geographically to another place rather than risk that new vision. It wasn't a wise decision or an easy time. Joppa and Tarshish didn't work for me either.

Years ago, a client shared with me an active imagination exercise, wherein he entered a special castle. He had to enter by getting down low and crawling on his belly under the barrier. Inside he encountered two doors. The first was a colourful entry outlined in flashing lights. He opened it and found an escalator going down. He got on and started down, but then saw that it was utterly dark below him and there was no escalator coming up, so he dashed quickly back up the down escalator into the hall. The second door was a plain wooden door with no decoration or design. He opened it and found himself in a large forest area in the centre of which he encountered an angelic being who engaged him in a simple and very touching ritual of blessing. From there the challenges began. We are reminded to beware of the attractive alternative. Sometimes the harder option is the better one. Heller informs us that, the literal meaning of the names of the cities Joppa and Tarshish, are 'beauty' and 'wealth.'[4] How amazing; that's not even subtle! We sometimes resist, we seek to avoid the challenges of divinity, wisdom, and seek distractions and attractive alternatives in all manner of ways and places. James Hollis offers an interesting list of what we might label the spiritualities of distraction, and they do abound.[5]

Paul Murray, in his little book, *Journey with Jonah*,[6] also affirms that Jonah's story is our story, and that sooner or later we will be challenged to face up to a "Nineveh" of our own. We will be summoned. A claim will be made on us for our time, on our capacity to love, on our courage, or perhaps on our assets, or all this and more. It is a challenge we that we may well want to resist. Then comes the storm.

The Storm

The text reads, "… the LORD, hurled a great wind upon the sea, and such a mighty storm came upon the sea that the ship threatened to break up." (Jonah 1:4) "Go to Nineveh," and Jonah heads for Joppa and Tarshish. Resistance for Jonah leads to the storm, the crisis. On casual reflection I would have seen the belly as the crisis, but now assert that the storm is the crisis. The storm is pivotal to the story and to the process of alignment. The image of the storm reminds us again that the divinely driven process of transformational healing and wholeness, is not always a simple, straightforward, manageable, or pleasant experience. Eugene Peterson, in his work, *Under the Predictable Plant*,[7] sees the storm as wild and extravagant, beyond our control … The storm is all-encompassing and unmanageable. When it comes our way, we are fully in it, and sometimes it feels life threatening. It can feel like a life-or-death event. We are not spectators and in those moments nothing else seems to matter.

The image of the storm is an unnerving challenge. Why can't

things be easier? Is this the necessary road to our wholeness? Is the storm essential to the development of a mature and soulful spirit? It would seem so.

In the story of Jonah, the storm is the action of divinity. The divine life responds to Jonah's resistance with the fierce wind and howling sea. In reflecting on this in terms of our experiences, we may realise that we have a picture of God that no longer works for us. If we can shift our imaginations and consider the activity of the storm as a symbol of the deep and divine wisdom of our souls attempting to get us back on track, then perhaps we can engage the storm image deeply. Is there a wisdom, a divine and sacred wisdom, a godly voice deep within us that will cause havoc for us when we refuse and resist the divine summons? Out of my lived experience I will answer, "Yes." I first read Thomas Kelly's *A Testament of Devotion* over forty years ago. A passage at the beginning invites me to reflect on who I am and who speaks from the depths of my soul. Kelly writes: "Deep within us all there is an amazing inner sanctuary of the soul, a holy place, a Divine Center, a speaking Voice to which we may continuously return."[8] Influenced by Jung's notion of the Self, the archetype of wholeness, I conclude that the divine wisdom of the soul seeks nothing less than our wholeness regardless of the cost to us.

As we reflect on Jonah's story and consider our experiences as informed by this remarkable story, we need to remember that the insights and the pattern here may serve us sometimes, but not always. Someone long ago quipped to me that "always" is a four-letter word. Always does not always apply. As we seek to make use of this story, we also affirm that the individual storms of our lives are often very different in character, and not always simple repetitions of the Jonah experience. Generally speaking, the storm or crisis is whatever experience we have that causes us to begin to fall apart, to come unstuck, to unravel, to fall to our knees, or to find ourselves in danger. By and large the storm is a serious wounding experience. How we define and imagine the presence of the divine life in each of our experiences will differ greatly. Our questions might be something like these: What is the function of my soul's divine wisdom here and now as the deep seas rage and foam? What does my soul want from me when I feel overwhelmed by one stormy crisis or another? Where is my God in my stormy experience?

For me there are some life examples. At age 22, I received the diagnosis of a lower back condition which was from birth. Surgery was not advised. I was challenged to take physical care and to make peace with my condition. I did not feel aligned, I had no desire to embrace the summons to a new self-understanding and to new physical limits. I was thrown into a deep and long crisis about my life, my limits, and my relationship with my God. Out of that long deep-sea experience, I still do not see my God, the divine wisdom, as having caused the physical condition with which I was, and am, challenged to live. Rather I have experienced this divine life as an intimate companion as I learned to accept and live within the limits life gives me. The storm was a response to my inability at the outset to accept my life as it was and now is. The divine life, my God, was and is companion to me in living with my limits, including my times of pain.

With the alcohol it was different. I can accept that God, the divine energy, the wisdom of the soul, put rocks and stones in my path as I continued to resist and deny my addiction. I can see now that the issue had to be forced in some way, and I am thankful that I took the warning sooner rather than later. I need to remind myself that this divine wisdom of the soul wants nothing less than my best and whole being to emerge in this life, regardless of the cost to my sometimes resistant self.

The Jonah Syndrome: Do You Get It?

At age 33, in an unexpected movement one morning, I bumped my Adam's apple and could not speak above a whisper. It was awkward and unnerving to say the least. Three days later a chiropractor adjusted the cartilage in my throat into place and within hours waves of anxiety and depression settled in for a stay. I did not see this storm coming, and only came much later to see that I was so ego driven at that time with my performance and my public image, that I didn't even hear a call to Nineveh, or notice any response of resistance. I stood in our kitchen that morning, after my throat had settled, trembling with fear as the storm-like unconscious energies announced their presence. I struggled with anxiety and depression for about six months. I came to accept that divinity was at the core of this unusual experience that surely got my attention. I was way off the track living a life of self-conscious performance and seeking the approval and love of others to an injurious degree. My God, the divine wisdom was my companion through some difficult days and nights on the way to a new sense of self. Sometimes it is hard to get my attention.

In Jonah's crisis experience on the ship, there are wonderful literary details that heighten the drama of the story. The images of "down" dramatize Jonah's experience: down to Joppa, down into the ship's hold, down to rest, down into sleep, down into a trance. Down he went. When confronted by the sailors as the one causing the storm, Jonah reveals that he knows who he is in relationship to his God. He knows he is on the run, and it doesn't seem to have occurred to our Jonah that he was endangering others in his flight. This alone is worth a careful reflection. How do my life choices affect not only me but others, the others in my inner village and others around me in life? Also, he knows what must happen to calm the storm and save the others. The "down" continues when Jonah is thrown down into the stormy sea and sinks down into its depths only to be taken down into the belly of the great fish. Resistance, it seems, can take us down a long way.

The text reads: "Pick me up and throw me into the sea; then the sea will quiet down for you … " (Jonah 1:12) Note that before they do this, the sailors first try to row toward land to put Jonah off safely. Their concern for Jonah is in dramatic contrast to his earlier lack of concern for them.

Surrender

Here is a turning point for Jonah, he surrenders. He knows that he must go overboard to save the others. He knows that he cannot escape his God who now pursues him. He knows he will have to give in. A man shared a dream with me years ago that is about surrender. Here is the dream of the snake in the chook pen.

I wake from sleep and walk into the yard. I am now in an old disused chook pen. The floor of the pen is deep in litter, old, dry, dusty earth, feathers, bones. I am on my hands and knees as the roof of the coop is too low to allow me to stand. I see a hole in the corner, and I think of rats. I think again, aware of the presence behind me. No, a snake lives, comes out of that hole. In spite of my rising apprehension, I turn to face whatever is behind me.

A large (over two metres) red snake, as thick as my arm. I can see that it is no ordinary snake. Its skin is shiny, no scales, it looks like red agate, polished, alive. I can see right into it, but not through it. My first impulse it to seize it, strangle it. I cannot run, it stands between me and the door. Some instinct makes me calmly stretch out my legs in a sitting position, my arms supporting my torso at a slight reclining attitude. I notice that I am naked.

The snake slides towards me, over my thighs, encircles my chest. Its head rises to face me. I am aware that the snake rests on my penis. Although it is not erect, I am aware that it is full of life. Similarly, it touches my chest over my heart. I look the snake in the eye, more in awe than in fear. 'I am keeping an eye on you.' Who speaks I am not sure.

Amid all the interesting details in this dream, note the moment of surrender. "Some instinct makes me calmly stretch out my legs in a sitting position, my arms supporting my torso at a slight reclining attitude. I notice that I am naked." The physical position of the dreamer leaves him without defence. He surrenders to the visitation of the agate snake. This dream was a turning point in this man's soul work. He realised it was time to take the work more seriously. In a sense he was summoned to pay attention and surrender to the process.

Jonah, after being wakened and confronted, and after declaring the truth of his identity, surrenders to the process in the face of the crisis caused by the storm. "Pick me up and throw me into the sea; then the sea will quiet down for you …" (Jonah 1:12) In the face of any crisis there needs to be a moment of surrender to the process regardless of how it came about. We must choose to surrender to our crises and make decisions as to how to engage them. Avoidance and denial are costly decisions and through them nothing is transformed. The choice to surrender is essential to move Jonah's story forward, and in our crises to move us forward as well.

Self-sacrifice

Jonah's surrender then manifests itself in an act of self-sacrifice. He knows that he must go over the side and down into the deep to save the others. It is interesting to note that he cannot initiate this action and jump into the sea. He needs the crew to throw him overboard and into the next phase of his adventure in his relationship with his God.

As we reflect on our times of crisis, our storms, we must determine the self-sacrifice that we must make. Our present ego conscious point of view, strong, wilful, well thought out and defended, must give way, must surrender, to the new direction, to a new sense of self, and to the new demands and challenges of a larger life and a deeper truth. This self-sacrifice involves a symbolic "death" for the ego. Egocide, it is about egocide, that is, to choose to submit, to surrender to a deeper will or truth, and a new way to live.

I am greatly interested in the image of egocide that I found in an online interview with David Rosen, a Jungian Analyst. The article is entitled "*The Evolution of a Jungian Shaman.*"[9] As I have thought about it, I have concluded that many suicides may well be tragic, literal responses to a metaphoric psycho-spiritual impulse. It is important to consider that suicidal ideation may well be a metaphoric recognition that something needs to die in terms of our ego conscious understanding of our lives. A change is needed, but when literalised, tragically it may lead to an ending. Marion Woodman, another Jungian Analyst, addresses this matter in reference to adolescent girls dealing with anorexia.[10] She asserts that adolescent girls are often so enmeshed in the literalism of our western materialistic culture that they cannot make a distinction between a literal death and a symbolic death. While they may know a sacrifice is required to effect change, they must be helped to see that their literal death is not the solution. This inability to reflect symbolically on our lives and our actions is a deeply serious problem in our culture and inhibits our capacity to identify the appropriate symbolic sacrifices needed to effect personal transformation.

In my encounter with my alcohol addiction, I can see that choosing sobriety was a necessary act of egocide. It is fair to admit that in those early days, suicidal images did wander through my consciousness. I would suggest that some form of egocide is a necessary passage whenever we engage a significant change in our self-understanding. Something in my consciousness must "die" when I admit the truth of my shadow projection onto someone else, when I change my mind about a social issue, when I acknowledge my aging and the diminishing of my energies, when I undertake to change careers, when I experience the ending, or beginning, or the changing of a relationship, when I realise that I am not in control, and when I accept that I am not always going to get my way. All these experiences involve self-sacrifice, and egocide. Sometimes we jump overboard into the new, other times someone must throw us over the side.

Jonah heard the challenge of his God. He could not align himself with the summons to go to Nineveh but resisted and headed off for the distractions of beauty and wealth, Joppa and Tarshish. He fled the One he had previously sought to serve and love and ended up in a life-threatening storm that finally caused him to surrender and make self-sacrifice. Jonah is flung down into the depths of the sea and ends up in the belly of the great fish and his adventure continues.

The Belly

Enwombment

"But the LORD provided a large fish to swallow up Jonah; and Jonah was in the belly of the fish for three days and three nights."

Jonah 1:17

There is a change now in the whole dynamic of the story. In the crisis that is the storm, there is action. Scenes change, people are involved, there is drama, movement, and action on which to attend. The action in the story now stops, except for Jonah being swallowed and later vomited up at the end. We encounter Jonah in the belly of the great fish for three days and nights. Jonah is alone, alone with his God. He has known this God well, but now must learn some things anew, or be introduced to a deeper understanding of his previous knowledge.

I was not sure how to approach this image of the belly until I encountered a simple word change, a new image, in Jack Sasson's commentary.[11] Sasson refers to Jonah here as enwombed, not entombed. He is not dead, rather he is held in this unusual place for an indeterminate time. Jonah is enwombed. This gives us a way forward that can be very fruitful.

The specific details of Jonah's enwombment are left vague in the story, and some speculations are amusing to say the least. Various commentators over time have placed Jonah in the stomach, the intestines and one even tries to shove him into the penis of the great fish. The lack of detail in the text invites us to focus again on the relationship between Jonah and his God as expressed in Jonah's prayer, which is referred to as the psalm of Jonah.

The Psalm-Prayer

The Hebrew text of this psalm-prayer as explored by Sasson has much subtle insight and imagery that we miss in the English, and that gives richness and depth to this experience and the relationship. The opening lines in Hebrew imply the idea that this affliction is of Jonah's own making. This alone is a substantial admission by Jonah. He acknowledges that he has had a hand in his own circumstance. This is a startling moment of honesty on Jonah's part.

Jonah equates the belly of the great fish with Sheol, and in the belly of great fish/Sheol he laments. Sheol is that imprecise place of the dead, considered to be so far from God that only God's mercy can release the grip of death that now holds Jonah. From Sheol, this farthest place away imaginable, he now calls to the One from whom he had fled. In this place of the dead, he realises that God is somehow present. Psalm 139:8 offers a parallel image of presence. "… If I make my bed in Sheol, you are there." In his fractured and dis-membered state, Jonah's reflection signals part of the re-membering of himself and remembering again to whom he belongs. This is part of Jonah's belly experience.

While this is an enwombment, it has the quality of death, or includes the demand for radical change, – egocide. Sasson sees it as a death experience with hope. From Sasson's reflections we learn that the sense of being cast into the depths was a protective, and not a threatening act. Thus, even as Jonah is thrown into the deep and swallowed by the great fish, he is under the protective care of God. The Biblical Psalm 139:7 reads: "Where can I go from your spirit? Or where can I flee from your presence?" Where indeed can we go? Are we sometimes saved in our lives by ending up in the belly of the great fish?

Many years ago, a man brought this simple dream, Fishing and the Brown Bear, to a session.

I am fishing off a jetty with my twelve-year-old son. A big brown bear swims by and gets out of the water onto the jetty, between us and the land. A massive and frightening creature, we are very frightened. But the bear indicates friendship, communicates a message: "Don't be afraid". Our fear dissipates; things are okay. Our fear changes to happiness and confidence.

In our reflections on the dream, we explored the symbols of the ocean, of fishing, and the age of his son. Then I asked him what the bear represented for him. He said without hesitation that the bear was his illness. It seemed a surprising association to make. He went on to explain that he had been in a job in another country wherein he was trying hard to revitalise a declining community, but those who had hired him for the position intended that he prepare the community to be disbanded. They had not communicated their expectations clearly and he was really struggling to revitalise the group. He slipped gradually into depression and finally left the position and returned to his homeland to begin to rebuild his life. On reflection, the bear for him was a symbol of his depression. At first the bear looked menacing, but then it became clear that the bear was his friend. The bear emerged from the deep water, the unconscious, to be friendly and supportive. The depression was his belly of the great fish, an illness that saved him from further mental and physical deterioration. He concluded that he had been under the protective care of his God. Many of us may find it a surprising experience to understand his point of view and may struggle to consider an illness or some experience of wounding as a friend. We seem prone to see illness as an adversary rather than as an advocate. While this cannot be applied to all cases of illness or any crisis – "always" is not always true – in this instance this man concluded that the illness, like the bear, was his friend and had saved his life.

The turning point for Jonah is expressed in chapter 2, verse 6. "I went down to the land whose bars closed upon me forever; yet you brought up my life from the Pit, O LORD my God." In the depths, at the very bottom, often in our most difficult moments, something may well shift. With the shift comes an awareness, an acknowledgement, perhaps even a confidence, that the relationship with divinity is still intact. Somehow, at the bottom, the opposite energy can begin to flow, and ever so slowly the direction begins to reverse from down to up. It seems a common way with us that often we need to come to a sense of the bottom, with nowhere else to go, before an almost pre-rational conviction kicks in that something other than us, which Jonah knows as his God, is present and part of the process, urging us now from down to up. In one of his remarkable poems about Jonah, Thomas John Carlisle ends the poem, "All it Took" with the simple words "… He reminded me, and I remembered Him. That was all it took."[12]

He reminded, and I remembered. In the belly of the great fish, at the bottom, we often remember what really matters to us. Jonah remembered who he was. The remembering parallels that famous story of the Prodigal Son in the Biblical book of Luke. In chapter 15:17 we read that the young man "came to himself" or "came to his senses" and made his way back home.

Here in the prayer-psalm we read at the end that vows are made on which Jonah intends to make good. We might see this as the beginning of some long-range planning on Jonah's part. What is most clear now is the shift, not the details of what will result from it.

The belly

Since this is also our story, what can we make of this for us? What for us is the belly of the great fish? What is an "in the belly" experience? When have I been in the belly of the great fish? It seems to me that the belly of the great fish can become a place and time of serious interior reflection. It is the place of inner work, sometimes hard and disciplined soul work. Joseph Campbell, in his conversations with Bill Moyers in *The Power of Myth*, remarks that, "the belly is the dark place where digestion takes place and new energy is created"[13] For us, the belly can be a symbol of gestation in the womb wherein we review critically, and let go of, the old and make way for the new, whatever that might mean in a particular situation. The belly then is the place of the birthing of new life that will move us beyond the crisis, and involves resolution, acceptance, and conscious intention in engaging a new direction entirely. As with Jonah, the belly for us may feel like a tight and cramped place, not very pleasant, even harsh. We will need, like Jonah, to be there for the right amount of time, for that is the meaning of the three days and nights. Jonah was there for as long as he had to be there.

The metaphor of the belly experience for us may apply to a wide variety of experiences. These can include a time in residential rehabilitation, or a short stay in hospital that invites us to rethink our lives. My two days in cardiac care many years ago had all hallmarks of being in the belly of the great fish. I had my crisis of stress, and then time alone to reflect on a new direction for my life. The belly may take the shape of a retreat that we organise, or it may come upon us rather suddenly like the ending of a relationship or job. In a wider frame of experience, it seems to me that belly experiences can also become a place that we move in and out of over a longer time, as in therapy, counselling, contemplative spiritual practice, spiritual direction, coaching or mentoring sessions. The essential character of the belly experience is the acknowledgement that our conscious point of view no longer serves us. We come to the bottom, to the ground, in our lives. Whatever shape it takes, we go down, down again, to reflect on the essentials, the priorities, and our deep and unresolved wounds. We remember again our long held secret dreams and aspirations, and the experiences that give meaning to our existence. Here at bottom, like Jonah, we also confront the mystery of the truth that somehow, we are not alone, no matter how alone we might feel from time to time. What matters further is that we remain in the belly for as long as it takes.

In other sacred biblical stories Jacob stays alone by the ford of the Jabbok (Genesis 32:24), Elijah hives off to the cave alone (1 Kings 19:1ff), and Jesus get driven out into the wilderness for serious conversation about his future (Matthew 4:1ff), each is there for as long as it takes.

Belly time is a time of change and transformation. Since this is so, it is useful to remember that in our sacred texts there are stories that also teach us that the sacred new sometimes must be protected in its early stages from the status quo voices formed in us by external influences that often object to new ways of life. These voices, the present power brokers governing daily life, often have no interest in anything new that might destabilise the present order and power dynamic. For this reason, Moses was hidden in the reeds along the river (Exodus 2:1ff), and Jesus was spirited off into Egypt by his parents (Matthew 2:13-15). It seems a common experience that new thoughts that challenge our present understanding, especially in psychological and spiritual matters, are rarely greeted with enthusiasm. A dream shared by a woman makes a similar point about protecting the new life. It is her dream of the green snake. It is a dream we have considered elsewhere.

> "I am a young woman and I live in a little house in the forest with an older woman, who is lovely, serene, about 30 and non-aggressive. She wears a lace cap and other old-fashioned clothes. Her body is not visible, only her lovely face.
>
> But there is some threat to us from people from an organisation close by, where I also worked. We didn't have any personal power, but the idea of the green snake seemed first to be given to us; we accepted, overjoyed, as it was a way, once and for all, to escape from and overcome the patriarchal male organisation which kept us prisoner.
>
> We were given the opportunity to watch the green snake be born; it was just about 6 inches long. We saw it with some awe and such joy, and then it slithered off to safety until it grew into full power. It went into trees and woods that were near our house so that the organisation couldn't find it. They wanted to find it and kill it; they didn't believe it was a magical snake with strong powers. They were frightened of it and sent a security guard to be on guard at our house at all times; they would change shifts. I locked and bolted the door with three locks so that they couldn't come in, and we would have our privacy with the snake when it came to dinner. I set the table with flowers and candles to make it beautiful for the snake. When the security guards saw it they couldn't believe that one would do this for a snake. They wondered why I held it in such esteem. By this time it had grown into a big green snake. With this support from the snake, we achieved freedom from the organisation, and some respect."

An essential response to the belly experience is to decide with intention how to integrate what is new for us. It is one thing to have an experience, it is another to integrate what insights or new attitudes have come our way. Like the women with the green snake, we must decide how to make use of the new, or risk losing the value and purpose of its having come to us in the first instance.

A part of Jonah's experience was to realise that he was never alone. He understood that his landing in the belly of the great fish was a saving gift from his God. This is a part of the belly experience that each of us comes to in our own time and our own way. In these present days, our understandings and interpretations of our worlds and our use of language may differ. For me it is a sign of rich wisdom and quiet humility to realise that we are not able to make sense of this life without a wider point of reference than ourselves. From whence comes the bear and the agate snake? How does the green snake appear? We may struggle with how to name it: the Unconscious, Divinity, God, the Universe, Nature, name it as we will, the belly experience invites us to realise that we, like Jonah, are never alone, and that a larger life energy acts with us, and at times acts on us and for us, to create the lives of meaning we desire. However we name it, we are in an ongoing relationship with this mysterious Other that Jonah knew as his God.

Among its many functions, I suggest that the belly is a time of "re-membering." We often feel dis-membered by the time we reach the belly and hit bottom. Belly time is a time of reawakening, reconstruction, reframing, reorganising, re-prioritising. As the poet John Thomas Carlisle has Jonah say, "He reminded me, and I remembered Him. That was all it took."[14] Time in the belly of the great fish challenges me to remember again just who I am, and how I am placed in this world. In the Christian classical tradition, St. Augustine's observation in the first chapter of his

Confessions, speaks to this aspect of the belly experience: "For you have made us for yourself and our heart is restless until it rests in you."[15] Augustine and others today suggest that we are wired for God or divinity – however named – and will know no deep rest until we understand who we are in this regard.

In Jonah's experience and in ours, belly time is about change. Things must change, this is the imperative of belly time. This is the hard work after the crisis. It is hard work often in cramped spaces, in time alone, in facing harsh, perhaps even unwelcome, truths. How shall I live, what disciplines will I, must I, undertake to honour this crisis – belly time, and risk becoming, yet again, a new person? Belly time is a time to re-frame my identity at a fundamental level, it is a time to consider who I am in relation to the larger life – divinity, it is a time to consider how and when to transform what is new into action. The belly is a time of values clarification, and a time to re-prioritise the values by which I choose to live. It is a time to ponder, "Where to from here?" It is a time to clarify the ethic by which I will conduct my life.

In the psalm-prayer Jonah made vows to be fulfilled over time. This extends our responses into a longer frame. How will I act to sustain the new life within me? What must I do? To reflect on such questions is to begin to care for the new sense of self that emerges out of the crisis, and to begin to integrate our experience. What must I do? How now shall I live? "How will align myself with that larger life that interacts with me for my well-being?" Jonah is then vomited out by the great fish and finds himself on dry land.

The Plant

And Again ...

Having been vomited out by the great fish, Jonah's journey begins again. It is a significant second start.[16] In the story there seems to be a difference between the two messages that Jonah is sent to deliver. In the first commission God requires Jonah to "Go at once to Nineveh, that great city, and cry out against it; for their wickedness has come up before me." (Jonah 1:2) The second commission is to "proclaim to it the message that I tell you." That message is "Forty days more, and Nineveh shall be overthrown." (Jonah 3:2-4) In comparing these commissions Sasson asserts that the first is a simple death sentence for Nineveh, with no hope of reprieve. The second however, is a specific message that leaves space and time for a response that could change things dramatically.

After all he has been through, Jonah finally goes to Nineveh and, after walking one day into Nineveh, that large city, he declares the message from God, "Forty days more, and Nineveh shall be overthrown." (Jonah 3:4). The story tells us that the Ninevites, believing in God, went into the high gear of repentance, with fasting, sackcloth and prayer declared for all citizens and animals! When God saw this display, God called off the disaster plan. Jonah was upset and dejected. It was not at all the result for which he hoped. He was holding out for the doom of the first message, and hoping to see his, and therefore God's, enemies destroyed. Jonah is so angry that he prays for his own death, and God asks him, "Is it right for you to be angry?" (Jonah 4:4)

Jonah goes out to a place just east of the city. He builds a shelter and sits beneath it to wait to see what will happen to Nineveh.

God then directs a plant to grow over the shelter to give shade to Jonah. We must assume that it is more adequate than the shelter Jonah made for himself. Jonah is delighted with the protection provided. Then God appoints a worm to attack the plant so that it withers, and God sent a fierce east wind, and hot morning sun to shine brightly and Jonah swoons in the heat to the point of wishing again for his death.

God then speaks with Jonah. God asks, "Is it right for you to be angry about the bush?" Jonah answers, "Yes, angry enough to die." God then speaks about the bush and poses the final question with which our story ends. "You are concerned about the bush, for which you did not labor and which you did not grow; it came into being in a night and perished in a night. And should I not be concerned about Nineveh, that great city, in which there are more than one hundred and twenty thousand persons who do not know their right hand from their left, and also many animals?" (Jonah 4:9-11).

The plant

I have chosen the plant as our third image to get us into a central place in the final scenes of this story. Sasson uses an approximate transcription of the Hebrew word for the plant, qiqayon, rather than getting lost in the effort to name specifically and accurately which ancient plant it may have been. Recent translators have generally settled for the climbing gourd or castor bean, but Sasson chooses to leave the image vague. This isn't after all about botany.[17]

When reading this part of the Jonah story, it can be troubling that God seems to be playing with Jonah. God provides the plant over whatever shelter Jonah has made for himself. Then God causes a worm to kill the plant and sets a hot wind and rising sun on him. I suggest that this section requires our sense of humour to be intact in order to read it with any sense of satisfaction. From my point of view, the author does have God play with Jonah, to challenge him to a new place of understanding. It seems to me that the plant experience is a tease, and it is a challenge to Jonah to consider his life in a much wider context. I remind us that the core of this story is about the relationship between God and Jonah. The plant image leads me to several considerations.

It isn't all about me

Just before Christmas one year a friend in the USA sent me an irreverent adaptation of famous Christmas carol titles, each designed for certain psychological conditions. My favourite is the carol for the narcissistic personality. It is "Hark! The herald angels sing … about me!" One thing Jonah learns in this experience is that it isn't just about him.

What goes on here is not just about Jonah. There is a sense in which there are two conversions, if you will, in this story. The first, in the belly of the great fish, is about Jonah and God. The second is about Jonah and God and the others – in this case the Ninevites, who live in that great city.

It seems to me that it is necessary to touch briefly on what we popularly name as narcissism in our present western culture. This might be named the "all about me" syndrome. When narcissism is actively present in our world view, others are easily excluded. Narcissism is not self-love, but rather a form of self-obsession. While self-care, self-protection and self-interest are essential to our wellbeing, the narcissistic Shadow side of these concerns often results in a lack of concern for others. The balance between self and others is a daily dance for the healthy soul, and my lived experience leads me to conclude that the music never stops. In this instance we might see this episode about the plant as the dance between self-care and the Common Good.

In the sphere of our relationship with our God, however named, exclusion of those who are different or who hold to different beliefs and practices, especially ones of which we disapprove, has long and deep roots as part of our heritage. To Jonah it was unthinkable that God could love Jonah's people and love their enemies as well. Such a perspective of exclusion makes it difficult to accept the integrity of diverse points of view. Jonah's God expresses an inclusive and welcoming attitude to those Others, whoever they may be. From where I sit, the narcissistic, "it's all about me," attitude is destructive to the health of soulful spiritualities, for both individuals and communities. It is also devastating to any person or groups of people who are the Others for us, and who fall outside my narrow range of interest and understandings about life.

Jonah is upset about the qiqayon plant, his lovely shade and shelter for which he did not labor or grow; God is concerned for all the people and the animals of Nineveh, that great city.

The mercy of God

Jonah comes face to face with God's indiscriminate mercy and forgiveness. It is a stunning, mind-boggling character of divinity as known among the people of God and those of the Way of Christ. Jonah is reminded, and so are we, that at the core our relationship with divinity is shrouded in mystery. Often we just do not understand and sometimes just don't get it. The God of Jonah does not behave according to Jonah's limited and exclusive beliefs … and the story is also about us.

Our sacred writings contain other texts that invite us to remember the gap between the mysterious ways of the God and our daily lives. In the book of Isaiah, chapter 55:8-9, God says: "For my thoughts are not your thoughts, nor are your ways my ways, says the Lord. For as the heavens are higher than the earth, so are my ways higher than your ways and my thoughts than your thoughts." In the book of Luke, Jesus uses the parable of the Good Samaritan to remind his listeners that compassion and holiness are found in "outsiders." Hanna Wolff, in her book, *Jesus the Therapist*, suggests that this parable challenges us to reinterpret radically the notion of neighbour to include everyone.[18] This is possible only when we work consciously and with intentions to withdraw our individual and tribal projections that we have put on others. The challenge to Jonah, and to us, is to give up the luxury of having enemies, and to put an end to the privilege of scapegoating. We are invited to become conscious of our Shadow projections onto others by which we have dehumanised and demeaned those who are, in truth, our neighbours, our brothers and sisters in the human enterprise. This is a sobering reminder.

"Here comes everybody," is a declaration often used in James Joyce's *Finnegan's Wake*, and becomes a key declaration for theologian Alan Jones of the radical, inclusive nature of community that we must embrace in our own time.[19] If I sit with this for just a moment in a quiet inner place, I hear a stampede of human feet coming my way and part of me wants to hide.

The open-ended story

For me, it is a sign of the greatness of this story that it ends with a question. It's almost like the author is saying to any who reads or hears the story: "Over to you, what do you think is Jonah's best response?" "Oh, and what about you?"

In his study on the story, Eugene Peterson concludes that Jonah has two opportunities to act on behalf of his God and he fails them both. In the first instance he refuses, and in the second he just doesn't get it.[20] We don't know what happened after that "divine" question. Jonah, after his flight toward Joppa and Tarshish, his confrontations on the ship, the storm, his being tossed overboard into a churning ocean, after having been saved from drowning in the belly of the great fish, after having helped save the people of Nineveh, that great city, who heeded his warning, after all this, Jonah still doesn't get it. What it seems he can't get is the unthinkable mercy of his God, the maddening, mind-boggling energy of love pulsing at the heart of being and life. Mystery, it is a mystery; God is a mystery to Jonah. Why can't God, my God, our God, hate our mutual enemies? This is a sobering confrontation for Jonah. It is a story about us, so it is a challenge for us as well. Perhaps there really is something to this unconditional love. Perhaps somehow, we can acknowledge and move beyond any and all transgressions, the transgressions of others and our transgressions as well, and come to embrace even the unlovable as our beloved.

For Peterson, the story brings us to the virtue of humility. He refers to humility here as a cheerful, and not a grovelling, experience. In reference to our wellbeing, I suggest that for many the notion of humility implies some sort of negative experience of ourselves, perhaps even a sign of weakness. From my experience humility develops in us naturally as part of our growing consciousness and self-awareness. Teresa of Avila in the 16th century reflected on humility in a way that I still find useful. She pointed out that true humility does not lead to a negative self-understanding or to anxiety and depression. Rather it "comes with peace, delight and calm."[21] Humility involves telling ourselves the truth as best we can and living with ourselves as we are at any given time. Humility includes naming our wounds, weaknesses, failings, and vulnerabilities, as well as our strengths, talents, abilities, and virtues. Humility develops from an honest self-understanding that also enables us to relax within the limits of our lives and to know some deep sense of serenity and rest.

Verse 12 in the brief Prayer of Manasseh[22] speaks to me of a humility that comes from an honest self-understanding. "I have sinned, O lord, I have sinned, and I acknowledge my transgressions." Another translation reads: "and I know my wickedness only too well." This is part of humility, knowing our own wickedness.

A useful language tool in learning to speak honestly of ourselves is to speak of parts of me, for we are each a bundle of complex and sometimes contradictory qualities. Part of me is kind, generous, accepting and patient. Part of me is mean, judgemental, short-tempered, demanding. We are the lot. Each of us can complete the list. Sometimes we get it and, like Jonah, sometimes we do not.

Conclusion

We don't really know whether Jonah ever got it or not. There he sits, under his shelter, with a shrivelled-up plant, in a fierce wind and the hot morning sun beating down, pondering the question put to him by God. "Well Jonah, what about the people and animals of Nineveh, that great city?" There we leave Jonah, and over to us.

The story of Jonah is a story about transformation. It deals with change and differences. It includes the summons to undertake something new and demanding; it involves the crisis when we hesitate or refuse. It may result in times of solitude, often in tight places, and unexpected insights when we hit bottom. Finally it confronts us with the challenge to initiate a new sense of self. It is a story about our individual unfolding lives, and it can happen in challenging relationships with others. The Jonah journey can happen many times in life as we contend with our unfolding relationship with the mystery of our God. We are initiated time and again into deeper dimensions of ourselves and our relationships with others.

We leave Jonah sitting there to ponder God's question. While it is his story, as Heller asserts it is also a story about us. So, what might the questions be for us?

>   When did I last choose Tarshish over Ninevah?
>   What's been my experience of the belly of the whale?
>   Do I have any sense of being held in a larger life?

>   Who are my Ninevites, my Others?
>   How do I respond to those who offend my sacred values?
>   Do I sometimes miss the point?

>   Do I get it?

God speaks through the prophet saying:

> "For my thoughts are not your thoughts, nor are your ways my ways, says the Lord. For as the heavens are higher than the earth, so are my ways higher than your ways, and my thoughts than your thoughts."

Isaiah 55:8-9

Jesus turns to his disciples and asks: "Do you still not perceive or understand?"

Mark 8:17

Endnotes

1. Heller, Tzipporah. *Jonah and the Whale*, p. 1.
2. James, William. *The Varieties of Religious Experience*. p. 53.
3. Edinger, Edward. *Ego and Archetype*. p. 70.
4. Heller, *Op Cit.* p. 4.
5. Hollis, James. *Hauntings*. p. 105.
6. Murray, Paul. *A Journey with Jonah*. p. 16.
7. Peterson, Eugene. *Under the Predictable Plant*. p. 68.
8. Kelly, Thomas. *A Testament of Devotion*. p. 29.
9. Rosen, David. *The Evolution of a Jungian Shaman.*
10. Bly, Robert and Woodman, Marion. *The Maiden King.* p. 182.
11. Sasson, Jack. "Jonah" in *The Anchor Bible*. Vol 24B. p. 157.
12. Carlisle, Thomas John. "All it Took" in *You! Jonah!* p. 19.
13. Campbell, Joseph, and Moyers, Bill. *The Power of Myth.* p. 146.
14. Carlisle, *Loc. cit.*
15. Augustine, *Confessions*. p. 43.
16. Sasson, *Op cit.* p. 225.
17. Sasson, *Op cit.* p. 291–2.
18. Wolff, Hanna. *Jesus the Therapist*. p. 125.
19. Jones, Alan. *Reimagining Christianity*. p. 20
20. Peterson, Eugene, *Under the Predictable Plant*. p. 20
21. Teresa, *The Collected Works*, p. 189.
22. The Prayer of Manasseh is a brief Deuterocanonical work

included in the biblical collection. It is not in the Roman Catholic canon but is part of the Greek and Slavonic Bibles.

References

All Biblical citations are from the *New Revised Standard Version*, NRSV. 1989. Oxford: Oxford University Press.

———. *The New Testament and Psalms: An Inclusive Version*. Victor Roland Gold and others, Editors. Oxford: Oxford University Press.

———. (nd). *Work in Progress: Book of Jonah: Depth-Psychological Interpretation*. Online at: www.israjung.co.il/gustava.htm

Augustine, 400/1960. *The Confessions*. John K. Ryan, Trans. New York: Image Books.

Avila, Teresa. 1566/1980. *The Collected Works of Teresa of Avila*, Volume Two. Kieran Kavanaugh, OCD., and Otilio Rodriguez, OCD., Translators. Washington: ICS Publications.

Bly, Robert, and Woodman, Marion. 1998. *The Maiden King: The Reunion of Masculine and Feminine*. New York: Henry Holt and Company.

Campbell, Joseph, and Moyers, Bill. 1988. *The Power of Myth*. New York: Doubleday.

Carlisle. Thomas John. 1968. *You! Jonah!* Grand Rapids: Wm. B. Eerdmans Publishing Company.

Edinger, E. 1972. *Ego and Archetype: Individuation and the Religious Function of the Psyche*. Baltimore: Penguin Books, Inc.

Heller, Tzipporah. nd. *Jonah and the Whale*. Online at: www.aish.com/hhYomK/hhYomKDefault/Jonah_and_the_whale.asp

Hollis, James. 2013. *Hauntings: Dispelling the Ghosts Who Run Our Lives*. Asheville: Chiron Publications.

James, William. 1902/1985. *The Varieties of Religious Experience*. New York: Penguin Books.

Jones, Alan. 2005. *Reimagining Christianity: Reconnecting your spirit without disconnecting your mind*. Hoboken: John Wiley & Sons, Inc.

Kelly, Thomas. 1941. *A Testament of Devotion*. New York: Harper & Row Publishers.

Murray, Paul, OP. And Joseph Ratzinger. 2002. *A Journey with Jonah: The Spirituality of Bewilderment*. Dublin: the Columba Press.

Peterson, Eugene. 1992. *Under the Predictable Plant: An Exploration in Vocational Holiness*. Grand Rapids, William B. Eerdmans Publishing Company.

Rosen, David. 1999. *The Evolution of a Jungian Shaman*. Online at: www.cddc.vt.edu/host/weishaus/Interv/rosen.htm (Note: This site is no longer available. It can be found on The Jung Page. Org. The interview is between Joel Weishaus and David Rosen under the same title: "The Evolution of a Jungian Shaman.")

Sanford, John. 1970/1987. *The Kingdom Within: The Inner Meaning of Jesus' Sayings*. San Francisco: HarperSanFrancisco.

Sasson, Jack M. 1990. "Jonah." In *The Anchor Bible*, Vol. 24B. William Foxwell Albright and David Noel Freedman, General Editors. New York: Doubleday.

Sweeeney, Marvin A. 2000. "Jonah." In *The Twelve Prophets*, Volume 1. Berit Olam Studies in Hebrew Narrative & Poetry. David W. Cotter, OSB., Editor. Collegeville, Minn.: The Liturgical Press. pp. 303-334.

Wolff, Hanna. 1978. *Jesus the Therapist*. Oak Park: Myer-Stone Books.

The Initiated Male: What about Me?

Reflections on the Experience of Initiation

> The following material was originally presented from notes at a workshop for men in March 2008. This included the presentations and times for men to share with one another in small groups and over lunch. The day ended with a ritual of blessing for any who wished to participate. The blessing form is included at the end. The reformatting has involved some editing and the addition of endnotes and references.

The stages

We begin our reflection on the experience of male initiation by considering the various stages of a traditional initiation experience. Various authors identify them differently. James Hollis, in his work *Under Saturn's Shadow*, sets out six parts to the traditional initiation event. These are: Separation, Death, Rebirth, Teaching, Ordeal, and Return.[1] Mircea Eliade in referring to the

Karadjeri People of Australia, identifies three phases: twelve years, becoming a blood brother; fifteen-sixteen years, being circumcised and nineteen+, being initiated into the mysteries and sacred places of the People.[2] Arnold van Genne names three phases: Separation, Transition and Reintegration.[3] Richard Rohr in his work, *Adam's Return*, identifies four stages of initiation. Separation, a threshold space, a numinous encounter and the return to the community.[4]

There is significant overlap here among the writers, and we'll review the six stages as set out by Hollis. Since we do not have traditional initiation experiences available in contemporary cultures, we will be watching for ways we are able to connect in our own lives to these traditional stages.

The key element of the first stage of **Separation** is surprise. The young men being initiated are most often taken by surprise, and even taken by force, to go with the elders against their will. It can be a terrifying experience for those being initiated. In the cultures it is seen as the action of the gods acting through the male elders. The boys are "kidnapped" by the gods. From the outset initiation is seen as a sacred experience. In some instances, the mothers put on a dramatic display of emotion at the "surprising" separation from their boys. In the Biblical book of Jonah, we see initiation themes in Jonah's experience. Jonah flees from the task set before him by God and is surprised by the storm that interrupts his plans. Jonah sleeps through part of the storm, until his shipmates decide he is the problem. They realise they need him off the ship, and when their efforts to put him off onto land fail, they throw him overboard. What he could not do, they did for him. His initiation continues in a remarkable story.

The surprise factor can still happen today. At times we may hear men lament: "I had no idea what I was getting myself into," or "If I had known in advance what this was really like, I wouldn't have undertaken this project," or "How did I get into this?" Of course, we never know in advance what lies ahead, and this surprise factor can fulfil the archetypal nature of initiation as surprise. It is an experience that captures us, or kidnaps us, rather than being an experience we choose.

The first stage of separation in the initiation experience can be seriously disrupting of our current sense of self and of life. It is meant to reduce us to our essential character once again and to prepare us to enter a transformative journey in which all is up for grabs. For the boy, and for many men, it is the separation from a dependence on the mother or protective parent, and from a limited self-understanding that may be inhibiting the development and expression of our gifts, skills, and talents. It can also be a separation from the delusion that all that matters in life is us, and it opens us to a more comprehensive understanding of our shared life. It is the beginning of a journey of deep change into a more complete sense of being a man in our own unique expression. The separation is a dramatic first step, when something takes us into a discovery of a more complete self.

The second stage is **Death**. It is, of course, an encounter with death in a symbolic way and is integral to any initiatory rite. Something in us must die. Most often it is the essential nature of our identity that must change. This symbolic death includes pain, wounding, deprivation, and suffering. In the Christian faith tradition, it connects to the mysterious truth of transformation in the death and resurrection cycle as seen in Jesus as the Christ. In a wider sense it is grounded in the natural rhythm of the changes that we see in nature through the never-ending movement from dark to light and to dark again, the shifting of seasons, the life cycles of vegetation, flowers, grains, trees, and the natural life cycles of our animal sisters and brothers and of our loved ones and of ourselves. As a wider container or context, these natural cycles can give initiates a sense of hope as the death stage makes its demands on us.

For me this death stage came on in full force when I finally surrendered to the truth of my addiction to alcohol and made the painful choice for abstention and sobriety. It also came shrouded in uncertainty when years ago I entered a sudden downturn into depression. I have seen the death stage descend on men whose relationships come to an end and they are left alone. It was the case for me when I became widowed. I entered an initiatory experience that was not of my choosing but became my responsibility. The death stage makes it clear that something in us must die: our self-understanding, our identity, and our way of seeing the world, are no longer adequate to life's summons. We die to an old ego stance in life, we die to the delusion that we control life, we die to the idea that we are the centre of our worlds. We are pruned back to our essential self, and in a sense start life over again. It is interesting to note that one writer stresses that certain Greek rites included financial commitments that were sacrificial. In our contemporary culture that often defines money as the bottom line, this sacrificial aspect of the death experience could hold substantial transformative power for us. In this second stage we die in some way, we surrender to some energy or process that we do not control, and this leads us forward in the initiation journey.

The third element of initiation as Hollis sets it out is the experience of **Rebirth**. In this stage we see clearly that the dynamic movement of initiation is forward. There is no going back; there is no return to business as usual. The initiated man enters now a conscious and intentional process of change. The changes involve not only how a young man thinks, but how he lives and acts as well. Initiation has the capacity to impact the entire landscape of a man's life. In some traditional initiation rituals, the young men take, or are given, a new name. I read an account of one ritual in which the young men no longer interacted with their mothers when they returned to the community. Symbolically they left their childhood behind and joined the world of men. In my experience I have known three men who changed their given names because of a deeply significant experience that was for them an initiation.

In the Christian pattern of death and resurrection we find this same archetypal dynamic movement forward. It is important to note that resurrection implies deep change, the raising of something or someone new. Resurrection is not resuscitation; it is not a return to life as it was, but an adventure into what life will now become.

The fourth part of the initiation experience is the **Teaching**. It may happen all through the process; it involves learning about oneself, and about how to conduct oneself in the community. In a sense it is about appropriate citizenship and includes the practical matters that help a young man get along in the community. In a traditional context the teaching also has a spiritual aspect. The young learn the cosmological stories and mysteries of the people, and the sacred traditions and rituals that connect the people to the wider unseen world. These young men come to know their place in the universe and learn how to participate in the sacred rituals that create a sense of meaning for the people.

The teaching aspect of initiation is different from our modern secular forms of education, though contemporary school education programs often include significant aspects of socialisation and practical cultural components. The traditional initiation experiences are sacred in their intent and open the initiated ones into a wider world than their former familial or local community containers. In contemporary forms for adults, ongoing experiences of spiritual direction, regular spiritual practices, individual counselling, and groups dedicated to self-awareness and well-being provide guidance in learning how to live in a wider world frame. The teaching aspect of initiation can be long term in the initiate's life, extending far beyond the initiation event.

The stages of the **Ordeal** and of **Death** may be one and the same experience or be closely connected. These six stages are not in some rigid, sequential order. In traditional initiation rituals an important underlying intent is to assist the young boys to make the necessary separation from the domestic world as they engage the world of men in the larger community. There is a wounding in the process on some level for the young ones as they step into a new identity. The pain of the separation is part of this, and there may be other exercises that involve difficulty, danger, risks, endurance, and heroic action. These embody the Ordeal in such a way that the young men experience themselves differently. Embracing this new self can include letting go of old fears and growing into an expanded awareness of one's abilities, skills, and talents. There is a sense in which the Ordeal introduces a young man to a new and larger, stronger, and more independent sense of himself. He moves from boy to man.

The final stage is the **Return**. The boys return to the community as men. The experience of initiation is not an intellectual exercise, it is an embodied experience of moving through stages that lead to a deep transformation. In a real sense, the young men who return are not the same young boys who were taken away. The men return with a sense of place and purpose in the community, and with an experience of connection to the wider cosmic story that contains and holds the community. A sense of the sacred runs through the entire experience. The Return underscores the truth that the initiation rituals all happen in the wider context of community. While the boys each have their own experience, they often have it together, and it all happens in reference to life in the larger community. In this sense initiation is a communal experience and is critical to the health and wellbeing of the community. In the traditional setting the importance of community makes it clear that the initiated men, as individual men, still live out their lives in reference to the expectations and needs of the community.

In our time the phrase that we can use to capture something of this dynamic between the community and the individual is the "Common Good." We return from our various initiation experiences with something to offer others. If we can place ourselves in the wider cosmic frame, the offering of ourselves then involves our close community of loved ones, our local and national communities, the global family, and the entire creation. Clearly from our review of the traditional experiences we see that the return is not to some former state of normal, but it is forward into some new and more complete sense of ourselves as men with something unique to offer. Our commitment in our Return is to the Common Good as well as the individual path.

The Movement

In this brief review of Hollis' six stages of initiation, we see that the intentional movement is forward. The young boys are moving through experiences that are designed to bring them into a new sense of self as men, and to ground them with confidence in their communities. In the biblical tradition the movement of Spirit is decidedly forward. Any attempt to return to how life was before all this happened is a dead-end path. Forward is the essential character of nature and the natural movement of life physically and psychically. In the initiation rituals the boys move from their dependency on the domestic home life into the independence of adulthood. Their worlds expand to include the responsibilities of life as adults in the community. This involves a sense of being stewards of the land, of the cosmic stories of the People, and of the communal values of the culture. The initiated man lives within an interesting juxtaposition of images: he is a self-sufficient, autonomous man, AND yet utterly dependent upon the community and the larger cosmic life.

There are some who would interpret the "from – to" movement as being from the feminine to the masculine. Some draw a further parallel with these and assert that initiation is from the feminine and maternal – nature, to the masculine and manly – culture. I would suggest that we tread very carefully here. The traditional initiation experience might well have been from the hearth of the home to duties in community, and to becoming a keeper of sacred stories, but the feminine is also connected to the wellbeing of culture, and the masculine is also intimately connected to the home and to nature. In the latter case, many today would assert that a man has much to learn from his physical nature, his body, about being a man in the deepest sense of the word. This is a complex issue inviting open ended reflection. I suggest that more is gained by seeing these two archetypal energies as deeply integrated in the souls of initiation candidates, than is learned by separating them into some sequential process. Regardless of the language and images we use to speak of the initiation experience, it is a movement forward.

In terms of our contemporary experience, while traditional initiation rituals were usually collective group experiences, many men today will go through initiatory experiences alone. This often requires a greater struggle for men to become conscious of their specific experiences as initiatory in nature. It also raises the issue of collegial support men can offer each other as they find friends engaging the experience. In addition to this opportunity to support each other in these experiences, there is a possible collective initiatory dimension to experience that is important to explore. Sudden natural disasters are good examples of experiences that "kidnap" larger groups of people and challenge them, both men and women, to enter transformative experiences forward into something new. There is a collective dimension to experience that may be engaged positively by employing the template of initiation as a guide forward.

The Pattern

In traditional and indigenous communities, initiation was most often a one-off experience that established young men as adults in the community. For contemporary men the experience may be very different. Intentional ritual initiations by the community for adolescent boys largely do not happen. As I understand it, an exception to this is the bar mitzvah experience in the Jewish tradition. Yet men today at different times, at different stages and ages of life, can still be caught off guard, and be ushered into unexpected descents, "kidnappings" and separations. Each of these can have the markings of an initiation forward if we are able to reflect on them from this perspective. Each can be for a different purpose in order to address a different issue in our lives. The challenge for us is to employ the wisdom of the initiation pattern and apply the template to our experiences. The varieties of initiatory experiences are endlessly diverse and specific to each man.

Marie-Louise von Franz observes: "Every dark thing one falls into can be an initiation. To be initiated into a thing means to go into it."[5] From this perspective I will affirm that the experience of initiation is widespread, if not universal for men in contemporary cultures. The task then is to make use of these opportunities that come to us and engage with courage the various stages of the initiation pattern. We can learn to use the pattern as a template to understand and benefit from our experiences. As David Tacey asserts, we need to grasp the psychological, inward dimension of the process of initiation.[6] My concern is that if men do not engage these dark times in this way, they may fall into a sense of being victimized by others or by life, and for men this is a deep hole out of which to climb.

To engage the initiation pattern is not a call to war against an adversary, rather it is a call to engage the inner world of men. The challenge is to endure any difficulties and to learn from them, to ask questions about who one has been in the past and to imagine who one might become. The pattern invites men to reflect on life with others and to wonder how one is connected to a larger life than oneself. Richard Rohr says in summary: "Initiation is not about being a warrior, as much as it is about being conscious, awake, alert."[7]

Many years ago, a man came to see me in my counselling practice. I asked him what had brought him to this time and place, and he replied clearly, "my children." He stated that he did not want to pass on to his children the emotional baggage of the experiences he had endured. He intended to break the family cycle of patterns by engaging the counselling experience as an initiation forward into becoming someone new. Initiation offers men the opportunity to break old patterns and cycles for themselves, and for others as well. The movement forward carries the essence of a fresh start, a renewed beginning. There is a significant freedom that comes to men who can use the pattern of initiation in engaging the unexpected challenges of their lives.

Initiated into what?

The boys are initiated into men in the community. What does an initiated man look like? In my day asking a question like this was referred to as opening a can of worms. It seems true that traditional cultures that practiced intentional initiation rites would have had clear roles for the initiated man. For us, the days are long gone when we can point to one dominant overriding expression of masculinity – the manly man. While I subscribe to the notion that there are archetypal, transpersonal aspects of the masculine energy, families, cultures, faith traditions and ever-changing contemporary times all have input into what defines a man in any culture and in any age. Today it seems clear that archetypal qualities and social constructions combine to define an endless variety of masculinities. This is further complicated by the fact that cultures and even groups within cultures will differ as to what constitutes the ideal and mature man.

Perhaps the best we can say in this brief overview is that initiation experiences in our present culture offer us today opportunities to grow more fully into an expression of manliness that helps us express a more complete sense of ourselves, enables us to navigate the complexities of our cultures with some satisfaction, and presents us with opportunities to contribute to our cultures in authentic and meaningful ways.

There are two other matters here to consider. First, the pattern of initiation affirms that we are initiated into the future. The challenge here is to realise that we are each like pioneers in our own lives. Other men's stories and journeys may enrich and encourage us, but each of us must be prepared to explore and define our own path. We cannot step into another man's shoes. This can be a lonely journey. Tacey asserts that we will have to turn inward, father ourselves, and initiate ourselves largely through trial and error into a more mature psychic state.[8] Tacey is one writer who believes that many men in our time will need to undertake this journey in solitude and not in the company of other men. It is an initiation into a future, our individual futures in the context of our collective life.

Second, in our time initiation consciously seeks to separate masculinity from what we name as patriarchy. We affirm that our initiatory experiences today intentionally contribute to the ongoing deconstruction of the traditional white, heterosexual male dominated images of the mature man and leader and open us to an endless variety of masculinities and leadership styles. We experience our initiations today in an amazing cultural revolution that includes our growing commitments to gender respect and equality, to the acceptance of varieties of sexual preferences and identities, and to the celebrative reality that we are one human race, though with many cultural and ethnic variations.

Working in the context of the Christian faith tradition, Richard Rohr offers the pattern of Jesus as a perfect example of initiation. Rohr identifies five essential messages of initiation from the Jesus story. These are: life is hard; you are not that important; your life is not about you; you are not in control and you are going to die.[9] Rohr then balances each of these with a biblical reference from the Jesus tradition that sets the initiation experience in an affirming and intimate Christ centred context.[10]

The Initiated Male: What about Me?

Initiated by whom?

As I understand it, in traditional cultures young men were taken into the initiation experience by the male elders of the community. In our present time it is possible that a variety of different people and circumstances will instigate the initiation journey. This may happen by conscious intent or by an unconscious interaction. Most often it is older men who initiate the younger men. It can be one's own father, a grandfather or uncle, a mentor, a teacher or professor, a life coach, a boss or others in our individual stories. As an exception, Eugene Monick tells the story of being initiated by a younger male who at one point was his therapist.[11] His example highlights that many men today experience initiation through various forms of psychotherapy and counselling.

Women, especially the mother, can also set a man off on an initiation journey through a variety of exchanges. While it is from the mother that young men need to separate, it is important to recognise that mothers can often challenge a young man in such a way that he undertakes the initiation journey in response. To exclude women from this role is to risk demonising women. It is at times the mother or another woman who can inspire a man to his journey and periodically renew his commitment to the new and mature sense of himself that comes from the work. It is interesting that the muse in the lives of men involved in creative practices is most often feminine. "She"- the mother, a significant woman, and the muse, can provoke a man to a higher consciousness and a more complete awareness of himself.

A variety of events or circumstances can kick start the initiation adventure. For me it was a dream of an unexpected illness. In 1977 I was six months into a new job and already had some serious doubts about it all. I then had the dream. In the dream story I felt unwell, and my wife and I decided to visit a doctor. He examined me and told me that I had an infection in my testicles, and he intended to cut them off. I objected. He then told me he would give me one year to see if I could clear up the infection, and if I was not successful, he would do the surgery. That morning I told my wife the dream and we agreed that I needed to call a Jungian Analyst I knew to make an appointment. This began a five-year relationship and remarkable long-term changes.

The initiating event can be an accident that changes our abilities, or a diagnosis for ourselves or a loved one that dramatically alters the courses of our lives. It may be the start of a new job, an unexpected performance review, or a redundancy. It can be our graduation from a course of study or a geographical relocation. It may be a significant loss of any kind, and certainly the loss of a loved one. As von Franz states, any experience of falling into an unexpected and difficult place can begin the initiation journey.

The role of divinity – the Other?

And what of the Gods? In traditional cultures the energy of the gods stands behind the actions and intentions of the elders. Tacey, commenting on an Australian Aboriginal perspective, states: "According to this view, only spirit can induct us into a larger and greater world, and only spirit carries the authority that can lift us out of the landscape of childhood and move us toward maturity and self-validation."[12] For many men in the contemporary scene, the notion of God, however defined, may still be seen as the energy behind the initiation experience. The initiation experiences of such men may draw them into a deeper connection with the God and Christ images of their faith story. In this instance the death and resurrection cycle of the Christ story forms a container in which to interpret one's own experience.

It is also true that for many others the God and Christ images of faith traditions are no longer relevant and not consciously connected to the initiation process. In a psychological model some men may imagine the Other within, the wisdom of the soul, as the initiating energy. This awareness may also include a sense of submission of one's personal will to a deeper, more wise, and internal authority. The challenge presented here in contemporary culture is to recognise that initiation includes placing one's life at the service of something larger than oneself however this is imagined or named. It is part of the dynamic of Return in the traditional stages of the journey. To complete the cycle and to claim the ongoing benefits of the journey, an initiated man must locate, and submit to, an objective authority that is greater than the ego and that carries for him some sense of the sacred. In the initiation experience, a young man discovers himself and then places himself at the service of something greater. As Rohr asserts: "Initiation is a deep yes to otherness, instead of any superficial self-assertion or self-denial."[13] In reference to this, Tacey issues a warning to men. He asserts that if there is no larger "Other" that stands beyond the ego and gives a sense of a greater framework, the man's ego will attempt to fill this larger space, and that will lead to ego inflation, which cannot produce the increase of character that comes from initiation.[14]

As individual as the initiation experience is for a boy in a group or a man alone, this final question of service embedded in the Return is a key concern. Tacey, Hollis and Rohr are joined by others including William James and Parker Palmer in posing the essential question in a variety of ways: What or who do I serve? Another version of this is to ask: "What does life want of me?"

Rohr rightly asserts that my life, while unique, is ultimately not about me. My life is about us, and this is the longer-term issue the initiated man must address.

Conclusion

As we come to the end of these reflections there are several matters to consider that inform our understanding of initiation. The first is about control and is raised quite succinctly in a question by Alan Jones in his work, *Reimagining Christianity*. He asks: "What will you do, what sort of human being will you be when you realize that you are not in control and that you are marked for death? What kind of life will you choose to live while you still have time?"[15] The initiated man will begin to understand over time that, ultimately, he is not in control of his life. In our mortal and limited framework then there are serious questions to consider as to how we will live.

Second, the writers whose works I have referred to offer some cautions about contemporary involvements that may have some qualities of initiation in them, but in the end are inadequate. These include the experience of war, participation in sport, and success in the workplace. On the surface each may look useful in this endeavour, but each risks falling back into regressive and simplistic models of masculinity that ultimately do not result in a mature man grounded in himself, committed to his community and in service to a larger life.

Third, in our contemporary setting it is true that the one-to-one initiatory experience may well be mutual for both people. Regardless of the professional frame that surrounds the two, it is likely that each will gain from the encounters, and both will step into a larger sense of themselves.

It has been my intention in these reflections to address the question in the title: What about me? For countless years, initiation rituals for men have been essential and sacred aspects of traditional and indigenous cultures the world over. While it is not appropriate to try to replicate these traditional models, we can be greatly helped in our own lives by understanding them. Through an understanding of the initiation experience in our time, we can realise that our ordinary lives offer us experiences time and again that can initiate us into new and unexpected futures, and into a more complete sense of ourselves. Our task then is to reflect on our own lives and to engage our initiatory opportunities with a reverent and hopeful spirit.

Endnotes

1. Hollis, James. *Under Saturn's Shadow*, pp. 17–19.
2. Eliade, Mircea. in O'Connor, Peter. *The inner man.* pp. 29–30.
3. van Genne, A. in Tacey, David. *Remaking men.* p. 120.
4. Rohr, Richard. *Adam's return.* p. 31.
5. Bly, Robert., and Woodman, Marion. *The maiden king.* pp. 157–58.
6. Tacey, Op cit. p. 101–02.
7. Rohr, Op cit. p. 36.
8. Tacey, Op cit. p. 105.
9. Rohr, Op cit. pp. 32–33.
10. Ibid. pp. 153–166.
11. Monick, Eugene. 1991. *Castration and male rage.* p. 113.
12. Tacey, Op cit. p. 127.
13. Rohr, Op cit. p. 141.

14. Tacey, Op cit. p. 125.
15. Jones, Alan. *Reimagining Christianity*. p. 170.

References

Bly, Robert and Woodman, Marion. 1998. *The Maiden King: The Reunion of Masculine and Feminine*. New York: Henry Holt and Company.

Eliade, Mircea. 1958/2005. *Rites and Symbols of Initiation: The Mysteries of Birth and Rebirth*. Willard R. Trask, Translator. Putnam, Connecticut: Spring Publications, Inc.

Hollis, James. 1994. *Under Saturn's Shadow: The Wounding and Healing of Men*. Toronto: Inner City Books.

Hopcke, Robert. 1990. *Men's Dreams, Men's Healing*. Boston: Shambala.

Jones, Alan. 2005. *Reimagining Christianity: Reconnect our Spirit without Disconnecting your Mind*. Hoboken: John Wiley & Sons, Inc.

Monick, Eugene. 1987. *Phallos: Sacred Image of the Masculine*. Toronto: Inner City Books.

Monick, Eugene. 1991. *Castration and Male Rage: The Phallic Wound*. Toronto: Inner City Books.

O'Connor, Peter. 1993. *The Inner Man: Men, Myths and Dreams*. Sydney: Sun/Pan Macmillan Publishers.

O'Donohue, John. 2008. *To Bless the Space Between Us*. New York: Doubleday.

Rohr, Richard. 2004. *Adam's Return: The Five Promises of Male Initiation*. New York: The Crossroad Publishing Company.

Tacey, David. 1997. *Remaking Men: The Revolution in Masculinity*. Ringwood: Viking/Penguin Books Australia Ltd.

A blessing for men still being initiated

1. The man names those initiating events he has experienced.
2. (name), we give thanks with you for the initiating events you have already experienced.
3. I now anoint you and we bless you, that God will continue to initiate you into the fullness of your own unique being, and that God will also use you to bless others.
4. At the end, read the blessing, "At the threshold of manhood." found in O'Donohue, *The Bless the Space Between Us.* p. 65.

Images of Transformation

I do not remember when I first delivered the talk under this title. The notes from my files are dated 2014, but the original presentation was several years before that. I do remember that it was offered as part of a series of Saturday morning presentations that a friend had organised. With the help of a colleague who was present that morning I have put together the outline from which I now create this essay. While I have worked from the 2014 outline, I have done considerable editing. Since the original outline of notes is my primary resource, I am placing the essay in chronological order, 2014.

Introduction

After we had talked a while about the person known mutually to us, the psychologist asked me, "Do you think people change much?" I was taken aback, but finally replied that I did think it possible for people to change deeply. He listened to me and then responded by saying simply, "I don't think people change much at all." Our conversation ended shortly thereafter, and I realised as I left his office that I would not refer anyone to him. The conversation has stayed with me for a long time and continues to challenge me to affirm the capacity of people to change at deep levels of the soul.

It's not a radical declaration to claim that people change and do so many times across the life journey. The physical changes are obvious, the psycho-spiritual changes may be more subtle, often more gradual, and sometimes gentler in process, and not necessarily inevitable. Our lived evidence makes it clear that we do have the capacity to change.

It is also true that we often resist change. I have often told clients that I expect them to resist the processes of change in the psychotherapeutic adventure; to approach a pending change with caution and hesitation can be a sign of a certain wisdom. It is not always easy to embrace a future that we do not control and give in to a life energy that may sweep us along a pathway we had not intended.

William James, in *The Varieties of Religious Experience*, notes that any new idea is first experienced often as heresy.[1] The new can be experienced as an assault on our long-held and highly defended worldview. Often what first felt like an assault can be woven slowly into the tapestry of our life's understandings. While part of us may resist change and new ideas, part of us knows that life is also an impermanent adventure, and that change is one experience on which we can rely. Tukaram, an 17th century Indian mystic, declares in his poem *Certainty*, that "there is nothing in your life that will not change – especially your ideas of God." He goes on to declare that "Certainty can become an illness that creates hate and greed."[2] My initial remarks here about change are brief. As we begin, I affirm the complex nature of change and of our ambivalent responses to changes as we give our attention to images of transformation.

It is my intention in this reflection to consider five different images of transformation. Four of the five are explicitly drawn from the sacred texts of my Christian faith tradition. From where I experience and observe life, these images are counter-cultural in that they assume both the theme of death in some form, and the reality of our suffering as parts of the transformative experience. From my teenaged years I remember my mentor once saying to me, "Suffering equals maturity." It holds truth for me. These images overlap and are intertwined, and each gives us somewhat different ways to consider change and transformative experiences. Through our reflection on these images, my intention is to help us engage changes in our psycho-spiritual experiences in more creative and helpful ways. My hope is that these reflections will assist us to be more aware of the transformative and life enhancing energies in our experiences that enable us to embrace change.

The foundation for my reflections combines my involvements in a Christ centred faith tradition, and my lived experiences with the psychology of Carl Jung. The two for me are deeply intertwined into a psycho-spiritual framework, and I am grateful to both traditions that have helped me shape my worldview – my ever changing and adapting worldview.

Dying and Rising

Within the Christian Tradition the most well-known transformative image is the death and resurrection of Jesus. It includes his arrest, suffering, crucifixion, death, time in the tomb and resurrection. It is the cycle celebrated from Maundy Thursday through to Easter Day. It is an archetypal pattern of transformative change through dying to rising, cycling down and up, death and resurrection. Resurrection is not resuscitation; it represents the rising of an entirely new character, in this Christian story it is the Risen Christ. Some theologians assert that the divinity of Jesus begins with the resurrection.

As an archetypal pattern we find examples, or implied connections, elsewhere. Over fifty years ago, I read a commentary for a hexagram from the Chinese I Ching that began something like: "The way up often begins by going down." This is very common in traditional initiation rites, and we see it in the experience of Jonah in the belly of the whale. A young man once shared an active imagination experience wherein he had to crawl on his belly under the spiked gate at the entry of the castle in order to enter and begin his adventure. Dream stories often take the dreamer down into a cave or some underground place, even under the water to a place where the dreamer can breathe safely, as a prelude to encountering insight and wisdom, and entering a new phase of life. In the culture of AA and Twelve Step programs, the choice for sobriety is most often preceded by a downhill journey that will continue until the person "bottoms out," admits the problem, and chooses the way up. Down, then up.

The examples are endless, and the informing context in the Christian Tradition is the death and resurrection of Jesus, the Christ. It is important to emphasise that the one rising is not the same as the one who entered the way down. This is a journey of change. The journey down begins in realising the grip of addiction, facing an unexpected job end or change, and accepting the end of a relationship. It may begin with an unanticipated diagnosis, or the sudden loss of a loved one. These critical moments all initiate a journey down into an experience of the death of part of who we have been, and by enduring what we are summoned to do in the face of our crisis, a new sense of who we are now will begin to emerge. Down, then up. "We" who we have been, continues with us as part of our story and lived experience, but through engaging the cycle, we create the possibility of birthing new qualities, new perceptions, new behaviours, and new self-understandings.

The death and resurrection of Jesus becomes for us an effective model for transformative change. There is in the model a deep sense of hope. We are invited to trust the truth that if we will engage these journeys of change downward, at some point in our enduring work there will be a shift and we will begin to sense the coming of the new way. The model in Christ gives us hope. Another crucial quality of the model is contained in the wider context of love. The death and resurrection cycle for Jesus was an act of sacrificial love. We are challenged to catch the truth of this, and to choose to hold our experience and ourselves in that self-loving, sacrificial context. Our changes, regardless of the specific nature of the events, are opportunities to deepen our self-love and positive self-regard as we walk the path of transformation. Down, then up, as in the death and resurrection of Jesus as Christ.

The Dying Seed

This image of the seed dying comes from the Biblical book of John, chapter 12. Jesus is speaking and foreshadowing his death. Verse 24 gives us the image, here from the NRSV. "Very truly, I tell you, unless a grain of wheat falls into the earth and dies, it remains a single grain; but if it dies, it bears much fruit." Here we have an image from the garden, from the earth, that speaks of transformation through death. Anyone who has planted seeds and waited for the first sprouts of new life will connect to the truth of the process here. In reference to Jesus' death the faith community concludes that his seed-like death was of great benefit for countless others. The death of this single grain bears much fruit, even today.

How can we make use of this image for ourselves? Continuing with the garden imagery, we know that compost, manures, and mulches, old matters that are dying or have died, have nutritious benefit for the new life that comes. In my experience there has been great satisfaction when I have composted natural matter and then used this old rotten matter as a source of nutrients for the new plants. The old dies in the earth and nourishes the new that emerges.

In a psychotherapeutic frame it is possible to see this in the therapeutic relationship. There can be times when old things are giving way slowly and dying. On the surface it may appear that there is little going on in the sessions. One could conclude that the process is coming to an end. On one level that may be so, but through the dying of old ideas and behaviours the ground is being prepared quietly for the new life that will spring from the reflective dialogue with the unconscious. New insights, considerations, and energies may begin to appear like so many sprouts in the garden.

This image from nature also reminds us that some seeds die quite naturally. Over time we let go and give up on attitudes and behaviours that no longer serve us or in which we no longer find meaning. The fruit that is borne out of these natural transformations benefits us as we adapt to the natural changes that are written into the life cycle. Perhaps the mid-life transition is the most common example. At forty we do not live as though we were twenty-five unless we want to pay a very high price. As with plants, it seems for us that there are age-appropriate concerns, issues, and rhythms for creative living. I remember seeing photos of a female celebrity in her 70s dressed and posing as if in her 20s. It was simply sad. The natural processes of the garden do instruct us about the natural flow of human life. We benefit as do those around us when we let these natural transformations guide us.

Along with the natural process of things dying, this image can also imply conscious intention. At times we make a conscious decision to let go of something old and let it rot in the psyche. The decision to choose sobriety and to let go of addictive ways is an example once again. Likewise, so is the decision to let go of an aspiration or relationship that no longer is life-giving. We let the old dream go and as it slowly breaks down, new life and "much fruit" may begin to emerge. This image again rests on a foundation of hope. Anyone planting seeds knows the hope that gets us out to the garden daily to inspect the rows looking for the new life.

The dynamic of the seed dying and bearing much fruit applies not only to us personally, but also applies to our relationships with others. It seems appropriate to use the Jesus model here to affirm that our experiences of healing and transformation benefit not only us but benefit all those with whom we relate. Can we also extend this benefit out to see that our experiences of healing and transformation contribute to the common good? I chose sobriety years ago. The seeds of alcohol addiction and the practices of denial and avoidance, all slowly died. Along with me, countless others over years have benefited from this transformation and most knew nothing of my addiction story. Another common example helps us here: if I can choose self-care and bury the seeds of abusive overwork, my loved ones benefit with me, and it will contribute to the Common Good many times over. A seed dies and bears much fruit, perhaps in ways far beyond our conscious intent and understanding.

Pruning

The image of pruning gives us another garden image. It comes from the Biblical book of John as well, in chapter 15. It is found in the teaching about the vine and branches. The imagery here affirms that we are intimately connected to Christ, and a part of the larger God-human story. The image of the vine and branches is central to the claims of the mystical tradition that the Christ lives in us, and we live in the Christ. A vine and its branches are so intimately connected that one cannot see where one ends and the other begins. The image invites us to ponder our connection to a larger life, in this instance to a oneness with God in Christ.

Pruning as a transformative image of change is our focus here. The biblical text teaches that the pruning is done by God to cut from the vine what is not productive, and to encourage what is productive to produce more. It would be possible at this point to get side-tracked into a reflection on those branches that are cut out; this is for me a dead-end street that risks leading us into reflection that could become self-righteous and exclusive. There are other aspects of the image that are more beneficial when employed as insights to support our ongoing transformations into the fulness of ourselves.

How do we undertake the transformational experience of pruning for ourselves? There are three aspects of the pruning process that are useful for us. First, there are pruning changes initiated by life and exterior circumstances that summon us to the path of change. Second, pruning changes will emerge from the unconscious to assist us forward, even if this is painful. Third, there are pruning changes we choose consciously to undertake.

Years ago, I had lunch with a colleague who was in between job positions. He was squeezed out of the executive level of management through a merger of two companies. It was a surprise, and he was left to get on with things. He was clear in our conversation that the experience had given him reason to examine his life carefully as to what mattered most and where he wanted to position himself in the work force. Pruning by life or exterior circumstances often brings us to our essential ground, or as we sometimes say, back to square one. As we have seen already, these circumstances are many, including difficult medical news for us or a loved one, the ending of a relationship, or a geographical relocation. In recent years the global landscape has given us many experiences that have the potential to help us prune. The Covid pandemic, and the ongoing concern for a new normal has brought many to places of reflection on the essentials for a meaningful life. Natural disasters have done the same for many others as well. Raging bush fires, volcanic eruptions, and devastating floods have been more common than we would wish. When most people lose everything through these experiences the pruning requires deep reflection on what matters most and how to cultivate new growth forward based on our essential and core values. Life can prune us.

A few years ago, a young friend shared a challenge that came to him spontaneously in his journal writing time. The statement was simply: "Don't get busy, get deep." It was an invitation, a challenge, to prune. As with this young man, the unconscious speaks to us regularly. We receive the inner voice of wisdom when giving quiet attention to an insight, when attending to the symbols of our nightly dreams, when wondering why we get so angry at the behaviours and opinions of others, and when we are startled by creative and future possibilities for change. A voice of wisdom speaks from the unconscious that often invites us outside the box of our present lives and invites us to prune things away to make way for creative changes.

These two aspects of the pruning image remind us that we are not always in control of the life events that come our way, or of the insights that emerge from the unconscious in the forms of challenges and tasks forward. Our conscious control of our lives is limited. Life, inner and outer, at times prunes. These two aspects of our consideration invite us to remember that there are energies in the unconscious and in life at large that impact upon us apart from our conscious control. At times these two seem to come suddenly, like a self-pruning branch suddenly falling from a tree. While outwardly this is so, deeper reflection leads us to realise that some sudden changes from within are often conscious expressions of unconscious activity that has been gestating for a long time. We live in a larger life both around and within us that continually engages us. In the face of these experiences of pruning, our personal freedom lies in our responses. We have choices to make. What shall we do in the face of the pruning experiences that come our way?

About forty years ago I had a very significant conversation with the man who was my spiritual director. In the conversation I shared a vision of the work to which I felt strongly drawn as the focus for my life. He challenged me to be faithful to my vision once it became clear. It was a startling idea that had never occurred to me; be faithful to your vision. The next day I resigned from several involvements that did not support my aspirations toward that vision. From that point forward the vision of my work became the measure against which I assessed involvement with any new endeavour. I learned to prune out activities that did not assist me toward my vision.

While life and the unconscious will initiate pruning events, there are times when we choose consciously and deliberately to self-prune. My story of fidelity to the vision is an example. The choice may begin with such exclamations as: "I can't do this anymore;" "I've had enough;" "I quit;" and "I need to make a change." We give up smoking, we change the way we eat or drink, we stop serving others to the point of feeling exhausted, and we move away from relationships that no longer have any life in them. The examples are individual and endless. We choose to prune, cut out the dead wood; we trim a bit here and there to stimulate more growth. Just as in the garden with the vines and trees, these pruning experiences over time create and shape our way of being in the world.

Our pruning as part of our transformation includes identifying our sense of vocation and our personal priorities. Pruning as a conscious choice in response to life and our own unconscious, and pruning by our initiative are intentional acts to simplify and to keep the focus on what we see as the reason for our lives. We learn to say "no," we learn to close doors, we choose our focus for living, we let go of those things that do not serve our path into our more complete self. The intention of pruning also involves trimming what goes well so that it may flourish. We sometimes narrow the focus of our activities so that we concentrate on doing one or two things well, rather than spreading our energies over a larger assortment of interests and abilities. We trim things down to be faithful to a vision; we "get deep." Life prunes; the unconscious prunes; and we prune and continue to shape our lives through our ongoing changes.

Shedding

We shift our attention now to a very different image, shedding or letting go. It starts early, very early. Others shape us through their reactions, we mimic and mirror what we see, we learn early on which behaviours please and which displease. Little by little "we" emerge as we develop, starting with the "terrible twos," but we are largely shaped by those around us from our earliest days. While this will cause us frustrations as we develop into what Alan Jones referred to as our "unique and unrepeatable self," our own ego consciousness, that early and continued shaping helps us to step into the larger lives of family, schools, work places, cultures, and world. This shaping satisfies our deep archetypal need to belong, which is one of the fundamental urges of the psyche. The Zulu term "Ubuntu" affirms this basic truth for us. It is expressed in various ways: "I am a person because of you." It affirms that the context of our individual selves is in fact the larger community in which we live and belong. John Donne's famous statement, adapted, continues to carry truth: "No one is an island." This sense of being embodied in the community, this ubuntu, is life long and of precious value to us. While this is true, there is an ongoing tension in what I refer to as the dance between self and other with which we also live.

Another way of speaking about this is to see ourselves as a referential self when we are young and still largely shaped by the worlds around us. This image of a self that is defined from outside us is key to many of the issues that emerge in counselling and therapy sessions. The question is: "How do I be me in the midst of us?" In reference to the Covid world, one of my daughters offered this dynamic as the ongoing movement between me and we. The dance never ends. The task at some point is to move our focus from being referential to becoming self-referential. We acknowledge that we are different at times from others. We affirm our own points of view, we make our own decisions, and we will at times be counter cultural. We work to embody that unique and unrepeatable event that is us. James Hillman offers a third movement here. He asserts that we complete the circle when we choose to identify and commit to whatever it is in the larger life that we serve. This may be named as God, Buddha Mind, the Universe, the wisdom of the Unconscious, The World Soul, or Life. Whatever name we choose, we align our unique selves with something larger than ourselves, and we serve the purposes of that larger life. Once again, we are shaped and formed by something larger than our own sense of self, this time most often by conscious choice.

What has all this to do with shedding? My concern includes the emergence of the individual self from immersion in our cultural containers, and then making the commitment to that larger life that binds us to others in a conscious act of belonging. In these complex and overlapping movements we shed or let go naturally of beliefs, values, and behaviours that inhibit the emergence of our unique selves. I think the letting go happens often quite naturally. We lose interest in something; we find ourselves letting go of relationships that no longer fit in with our emerging self. There may be no drama here, no conscious decision. We may wake up one morning and find that we have simply moved on in the ever-changing landscape of our lives.

Some might describe this letting go as a shedding of the false self. I am not at all comfortable with this language. It implies a negative judgement I am not willing to make and may well support a sense of civil war in the soul that is not helpful. It is the persona that is continually being reshaped and I do not see the persona as false. My persona is my face of relatedness to the world, and it allows me to share with you in appropriate ways. I often see it as a process of diluting me to a tolerable degree so that people can put up with me. I am told I am a bit intense. This persona is not false, but a valued companion in my interactions with you – with the world. As I seek to be more deeply myself in my unique human expression, my persona will change. Aspects of my social self, my relational self will fall away and will get set aside as no longer useful. There is death here in the sense of diminished influence or importance, but not extinction or annihilation. All of who I am and have been remain with me in my history and in my village. The dynamic interplay into which we grow and live is between a socially determined self and a sense of our individual self. The persona is that socially determined self whose task it is to help us get along in our various worlds. Its core function is relatedness. I see it as a tool by which I can relate effectively with others.

The ongoing aspiration of transformative change for me is to grow into my unique self in the context of all of you. Self and other is the ongoing dance, and as I continue to dance, I shed and let go quite naturally of aspects of my life that no longer help me dance into my deepest self, the self who seeks to create and then share meaningful life with you.

Communing

While there are many practices of communing with the divine life through prayer and meditation, the central event on which this transformative image rests is the last meal Jesus had with his disciples before he was arrested and subsequently put to death as recounted in the Biblical books of Matthew, Mark, and Luke. In the Tradition it is the Last Supper. At the end of the meal the stories record variously the sharing of bread and wine as a symbol of Jesus' communion with his followers. The Holy Communion is a continuation of this sharing among followers today in the liturgical churches. While given various names and interpreted in different ways throughout history by the communities within the Christian Tradition, the essential focus is on communion with Christ through the sacred elements.

For the people of faith, the partaking of the sacred elements of bread and wine conveys a sense of communion with the divine, here specifically through Christ. The core focus is union with the divinity. The dynamic of change is experienced through a conscious sense of oneness with divinity and through a sense of the infusion of the divine energy into the soul. This communing, communion, is the heart of the mystical experience, an affirmation of the unbroken connection between the soul and divinity.

How is participation in these ritual meals transformative? In the sacred meal the person of faith meets the divine life in a moment of deep union. Communion means *union with*. We are reminded once again in that moment that we share in a life of love that is larger than our own. We are connected in those moments with the ground of our being, with the still point in our turning world, with the anchor that holds us steady as we navigate the adventures and mysteries of life. We connect again with the source of our meaning, with the energy, the life that helps us shape purpose for our living. The entire communion – union with – experience affirms again that love pulsates at the centre of our existence, and we are summoned in the moment of being held in love to surrender ourselves again to the challenges of being loving and humane people. Communion extends from those brief moments into the ongoing companionship we have with the divine life. Companion means *with bread*. We share bread together; it is a basic expression of companionship. The companionship with the divine life enlarges our capacity to be compassionate with ourselves and with other people. Compassion means *to suffer with*. From the intimacy of communion, the moments extend into an ongoing companionship that enables us to suffer with ourselves and with others for the Common Good. Communion, companionship, compassion, this is the transformative pattern emerging through participation in the sacred meal. It is also the pattern of transformation at the heart of our ongoing practices of prayer and meditation. Our ongoing participation in this sacred ritual meal and these practices becomes a steady process of being reminded of who we are, and of who we are summoned to be. Ongoing participation creates an unending experience of being renewed to the truth of our own lives and the truth of our unbroken union with the divine life, the Divine Love at the heart of our existence, and the heart of all creation.

The pattern is not automatic; this is not a mindless or sentimental exercise. It is possible to participate in the form and miss the substance. The efficacy of the transformative pattern depends on our attending upon the sacred ritual meal consciously and with intention to be open to commune again with the divine life in that ritual moment. In this we are renewed again to the truth of our unbroken union with divinity, and to our challenge to share from this union for the Common Good. Communion, companionship, compassion; this is the transformative experience possible through the sacred meal and our prayerful and meditative practices.

Conclusion

"Do you think people change much," he asked. Yes, I do, and these images of transformation help us understand various ways from the Christian faith tradition that this can unfold. Woven into these processes of change is the theme of death – something old gives way so that something new can emerge as a new way to be. Another theme woven into these changes is the notion of attitude. Many times the awareness that assists us in changing is the willingness to change our attitude toward whatever our issue happens to be. Transformative change often involves seeing our present circumstance from a different point of view. In many instances our external circumstance may not change dramatically, but the way we engage our lives in this instance may well open us to a deep sense of healing. To choose sobriety I had to change the attitude that deluded me into thinking I was in control of my alcohol intake. Once I realised I was not in control, my attitude changed toward myself, and my use of alcohol and I was free to choose sobriety as my new path. I still live with addictive tendencies (let's hear it for chocolate!) but the change of attitude toward this personality trait has transformed the way I live. Likewise, I had to change my attitude toward my life-long back condition. At first, I resented it. I felt really struck down and victimised by life. Once I changed my attitude and decided this condition was my companion that was not going to go away, a significant healing took place through my practices of self-care that have allowed me to live a full and interesting life, within certain limits.

A change of attitude, reframing our story, can support our transformation and deep healing. Over the years it has been my experience that this change of attitude opens us to the possibility of making use of our wounds to shape a more distinctive character.

I have learned it is wise to seek the blessing that can be hidden in our wounds, limits, struggles and difficulties. All this benefits us, but also enlarges our capacity to be of use to others who are summoned to walk through difficult times and circumstances.

These images of transformation provide us with models like signposts that can guide our individual soul's experiences of change. We walk the way of the cross, we bury the seed to die in hope of something new emerging, we prune away what no longer works for our benefit, we shed, we sluff off the old, and we commune in solitude with the divine life, who is our companion and who ignites our compassion. We learn to die; we learn to change our attitude and embrace the challenges of transformation. Through all these experiences there is still that remarkable sense of wonder at who we are and who we are summoned to be. Amid all the transformations into a more soulful and compassionate person, I find a comment of Jung's a helpful reminder. He observes in the prologue to *Memories, Dreams, Reflections*, "At bottom we never know how it has all come about."[3] At the heart of our ever-changing, transforming, lives there is great mystery.

Endnotes

1. James, William. *The Varieties of Religious Experience*. p. 335.
2. Tukaram. "Certainty." *Love Poems from God*. p. 350.
3. Jung, Carl. *Memories, Dreams, Reflections*. p. 4.

References

1. James, William. 1902/1985. *The Varieties of Religious Experience*. New York: Penguin Books.
2. Tukaram. "Certainty," in *Love Poems from God: Twelve Sacred Voices from the East and West*. Trans: Daniel Ladinsky. 2002. New York: Penguin Compass.
3. Jung, Carl. 1961. Aniela Jaffe, Ed. *Memories, Dreams, Reflections*. New York: Pantheon Books.

Creating Inclusive Organisations

In May 2019, I was asked by my colleague Dr. Stacie Chappell to participate as one of three speakers in a ninety-minute workshop at the Management, Spirituality and Religion Interest Group, in Boston, Massachusetts, on the topic, "Creating Inclusive Organisations." Because of the time difference, we agreed that I would send the following letter for her to read out to the participants. The workshop was on 12 August 2019. I have added the appropriate endnotes.

Dear Stacie:

First, thank you for the invitation to participate in this workshop "Creating Inclusive Organisations." From where I sit in life, this topic is out on the front edge of the movements that seek to reclaim the priority of people and their lives over all other organisational goals and purposes. I am much in favour of this.

As I have been reflecting on what I can offer you and the

others, I realise that my starting place is to affirm our complexity. The world in which I grew up in mid-twentieth century America seemed to value people who held simple, clear, direct points of view. Maturity was presented as clearly knowing one's opinion on most everything, and not wavering from it. It has become clear to me over the years that I do not stand in that tradition. Influenced deeply by the psychological work of Carl Jung from my teenage years, I value instead the complexity, ambivalence, the chaos, and contradictory natures of people. Maturity, for me, often means not being sure as to what to decide and how to act in the face of complex, layered and confusing issues. I am not single minded in my points of view, but rather play host to a wide variety of opinions and attitudes that often are at odds with each other. I am more like a collection of people with very diverse approaches to life's experiences.

Over the years I have come across remarks by various people who support this point of view. Richard Flanagan, an Australian author, commenting on the strength of the novel form of literature, observes, "It reminds us that each of us contains multitudes."[1] In his *Leaves of Grass*, Walt Whitman offers this:, "Do I contradict myself? Very well, I contradict myself, I am large, I contain multitudes."[2] The Irish theologian John O'Donohue describes us as having a crowd at the hearth of the soul.[3] James Hillman, an American Jungian Analyst, prefers to think of each of us like a boarding house,[4] often with some very strange characters living in the rooms upstairs and down at the end of the hall. Rumi, the Sufi mystic, offers us a poem in which we are each compared to a guesthouse, with different characters coming and going.[5]

In the development of my own reflections over the years, I have settled on the notion that each of us is like a village of diverse, interesting, and sometimes, unnerving people. The goal I hold for myself, and others is to come to make peace with and include all those inner characters, sub-personalities Hillman names them, as we come to know them. The goal is radical inclusivity.

How does this personal work of self-reflection have relevance to an inclusive organisation?

As you will remember Stacie, when you worked with Brendan McKeague and me on the Nonviolent Interfaith Leadership Conferences, we three worked long and hard in 2010 to distil from our experiences a series of principles that were the foundation of our work. One of these is "Our inner work shapes our outer lives." As I understand it, we were attempting to affirm that disciplined work of self-reflection is essential to a humane and nonviolent approach to ourselves and to others with whom we share the family, the workplace, the worship community, or any other gathering. It is my own experience that my inner work, especially coming to terms with the difficult parts of me, is essential to my being able to work humanely with others. To say it another way, if I do not love myself, I cannot sustain any love for you. The American theologian Richard Rohr says in various ways that what is not transformed within is transferred.[6] These words take us to the basic principle of negative projection that we will have encountered in any first semester study of psychology 101.

Recently a woman talked with me with some agitation about a woman she supervised in the workplace. It was not the first time we had been over this territory. At one point she sighed and said, "She represents everything I do not want to be." A classic negative projection, a "Shadow" projection as Jung would name it, and it set the woman up for a deeper self-understanding so that she could enter the relationship with the woman she supervised with more patience and compassion. Our inner work shapes our outer lives.

In my own principles developed from our work together, I remind myself that what I do not engage within I project onto others. Back in the early 1960s I read Jung's memoir, *Memories, Dreams, Reflections*. In it I came across this line that I have, much to my annoyance, memorised, "Everything that irritates about others can lead us to an understanding of ourselves."[7]

A young man in his late 30s shared with me an encounter with a man in his village named Rage. When I inquired as to how he wanted to proceed with this encounter, he said with force, "I want to punch his lights out." With further conversation, he came to admit that this would not help him in any way. He needed to make peace with his rage and understand his history and point of view so that he could come to terms of peace with himself. In the work mentioned above, John O'Donohue observes that so many of us live in a perpetual war zone within ourselves. Radical inclusivity, as a foundation for contributing to inclusive gatherings of any kind, requires us to come to make peace with ourselves. If I do not love me, what chance have I got of loving you?

By way of this long and rambling reflection I want to focus on the inner village and the goal of peace within as the starting place for building inclusive, humane organisations, gatherings of any kind.

Who's here? Who is in the village? For each of us this will be different. Often, we start with negative characters, but tucked away in the alleyways and side streets, we may also find others who are very positive; these are the unlived lives that we did not know, or that we choose not to express. In my village is a monk. I chose marriage instead, but he is still around and a helpful character in shaping my life as a widower. There are children in the village who remind me of significant moments along the way, there is my image of rage who can cut loose when I feel slighted and when I focus on the injustices of governments and other groups against vulnerable people. There is one who is generous and his mate, the selfish one. There is one needing attention who grew to life in my early years and is still around. I am amused at the Proper One, who loves to remind me to behave when I act like a jerk or cross socially acceptable forms and boundaries. There is one who tries too hard and one who takes good care of me. What a colourful cast of characters make up the Village of Trippe. An intellectual, a holy man, a lusty sleeze bag, an opera singer who never made it to the stage of the Metropolitan Opera, a young adventurer who is open to any new idea, a judgemental guy who knows with certainty that he is right. All these parts of me, and more make up what my kids refer to as their intense and complex dad.

In dealing with the inner villagers and negotiating relationships toward peace, the key phrase that has emerged in my experience is "part of me." So, instead of saying "I am angry," I can say "part of me is angry." This affirms that other parts of me may not be angry, and it minimises the experience of being overwhelmed by any specific attitude, rational opinion, or emotional response. "Part of me" creates a distance between my responses and me in such a way that I am free to choose how to engage the outside world. It also opens the door to the possibility of dialogue with those parts of us that are yet to be welcomed into the village and who may well be the cause of our tense and unhealthy reactions to others in the family, or the workplace or the faith community. Using one's imagination to have a talk with Rage or Needy can be a liberating experience that allows us to engage others with a greater patience and compassion.

In a short review I have tried here to cover a great and grand territory. So, let me summarise key points. To create inclusive organisations, we start with ourselves. We are complex, made of many diverse attitudes, opinions, and responses. Maturity involves embracing our complexity and diversity. Self-reflection is essential to any attempt to be inclusive. Radical inclusivity challenges us to engage and befriend all of us over time. The inner village helps us hold our complexity more effectively. "Part of me" as a verbal tool helps us carry our complexity with more ease. Inner work with the villagers enables us to be more compassionate with others.

Well, Stacie, I hope this is useful. If it keeps some awake at night wondering at the mystery of who we are, then I will be satisfied!

If any who hear this wish to communicate with me about any of this, please share my email address, georgetrippe@gmail.com. Best wishes to you as always and to the workshop participants.

George

Endnotes

1. Flanagan, Richard. 2017-18. *Underline.* p. 4.
2. Whitman, Walt. *Leaves of Grass.* Section 51. p. 83.
3. O'Donohue, John. *Anam Cara.* p. 113.
4. Hillman, James. *The Force of Character,* p. 32.
5. Rumi. *The Guesthouse.*
6. Rohr, Richard. *Adam's Return.* p. 37.
7. Jung, Carl G. *Memories, Dreams, Reflections.* p. 247.

References

Flanagan, Richard. 2017–18. "The truth is a story. An interview by Samson McDougall with Richard Flanagan." in *Underline*. Issue 5, Summer, 2017–18. Penguin Random House Australia.

Hillman, James. 1999. *The Force of Character and the Lasting Life*. New York: Random House.

Jung, Carl G. 1961. Aniela Jaffe, Ed. *Memories, Dreams, Reflections*. New York: Pantheon Books.

O'Donohue, John. 1997. *Anam Cara: A Book of Celtic Wisdom*. New York: Harper Perennial.

Rohr, Richard. 2004. *Adam's Return: The Five Promises of Male Initiation*. New York: A Crossroad Book.

Rumi. https://www.scottishpoetrylibrary.org.uk/poem/guest-house/. Listed on this website from *Rumi: Selected Poems*. 2004. Trans. Coleman Barks with John Moynce, A. J. Arberry, Reynold Nicholson. Penguin Books.

Whitman, Walt. "Song of Myself," in *Leaves of Grass*. San Diego: Canterbury Classics.

Stepping into the Christ myth

This essay is a personal reflection I undertook to help me prepare for the annual Christmas celebration in December 2021. This represents my attempt to understand the Christ archetype and myth embodied in Jesus of Nazareth, and the challenge to see in this a pattern for ourselves, without trying to replicate the historical figure of Jesus.

It was in late 1965 that I heard a presentation in which the speaker commented on the increasing interface between the Christian Christmas celebration and the retail world. He ended his remarks by wondering if we might someday be able to purchase a manger scene with a chimney on the stable. We all laughed, at what I am not sure.

Many years ago, an older woman we knew stated that she was not as interested in Jesus as she was in the Christ. Her own language was decidedly Christ centred. This made some sense to me then and over the years has remained a significant distinction.

In her very thoughtful study entitled *Jesus the Therapist*, Hanna Wolff has a biting critique on the contemporary Christmas celebration. She speaks of the cultus of the babe in the manger and reminds her readers that Jesus never asked to be honoured as a babe. She goes further to assert that the danger of such a focus constitutes a "great humiliation and castration of Christianity, where it has made it psychologically possible to glorify, and even dogmatize, one's own infantilism and immaturity."[1] Does the focus on the babe cause us to avoid the deeper meanings and significance of the birth of Jesus, the Incarnation?

John Sanford in his writing, *The Kingdom Within*, asserts that Christianity "... is not a sentimental religion, and the sentimentalizing of the feeling aspect of Christianity has been a disaster for the Christian spirit."[2] Yet our contemporary Christmas observances seem to drip with sentimentality.

While Wolff and Sanford raise valid concerns about the focus of our Christmas celebrations on the babe in the manger in western capitalist cultures, it is also true that the image of Christ as infant offers its own significant challenges. The essential quality of the image is vulnerability. A part of engaging the Christ image – of being Christ like – is to accept our vulnerability. This includes being vulnerable to myself and my needs, to others and their needs and stories, and to the world's pains and struggles. What is it like to experience empathy and compassion for the pain of others and for the planet? The infant Christ image challenges us to engage the pain of the world, of others, and our own pain, and to respond with compassion however and wherever possible.

Another aspect of the infant Christ image that challenges us is to realise how an infant quickly becomes the focus of the household. In ordinary circumstances, families of a newborn child are infant centred people. Routines of the home make way for the infant's needs. We go to great lengths to provide for our infant's care and safety. In terms of our spiritual relationship with the Christ energy within, how is this so? Is it so that the Christ, like the infant, becomes the centre of our souls and our daily lives?

More times than I can recount I have heard adults remark that Christmas is for children. What part is for children and what part is for adults seeking to engage the Christ Way? The Christ image is a complex one for us. It is of deep and important value in understanding how to embody the values of the Christ in our daily living. At the same time, it is important to critique the sentiment that surrounds the Christ image in contemporary western cultures today. There was no chimney on the manger. We are challenged to embrace the baby Jesus and the impact of the Christ myth on our lives, from a disciplined adult perspective.

In the context of myths as timeless truth telling, Carl Jung asserts in his memoir, *Memories, Dreams, Reflections*, that "… a myth is dead if it no longer lives and grows."[3] He proposes that the Christian myth, a timeless truth story woven throughout an historical narrative, must move forward or die. If a myth does not move forward, we end up with something that is more of a museum piece. What does it mean to move the Christ myth forward?

Jung, with others, works from a distinction between the fact of Jesus and the myth of the Christ. Some have expressed a distinction between the Jesus of history and the Christ of faith. This does not demean the historical figure of Jesus and the traditional theological claim that he is fully man, Jesus, and fully God, Christ. For Jung, to move the Christ myth forward means that we apply the Christ myth to our own lives. He states that this involves "… the self-realization of God in human form …"[4] not only in Jesus of Nazareth, but also forward now in us. Jung notes that this shift of focus was known in the early Christian movement. It is also a central theme all through the mystical writers of the Tradition. The Incarnation as a theological concept expands out from Jesus to encompass us. We shift our attention from a projected belief in Jesus as Christ out there, to include an internal experience of Christ within the individual soul. The Christ of faith enlarges to include the Christ of our soulful experience. Christ within us; the lively myth moves forward in us. In every generation we honour Jesus as our model for living, and our life task is the realisation of the Christ within us.

While what we have created in the celebration of Christmas may be for children, at its heart this Feast of the Incarnation has within its mystery a very adult agenda. The Incarnation affirms, radically, that the same Christ energy that was manifest in Jesus of Nazareth in history is at the heart of each of us, the Christ within, and it is our task in every generation to live our lives from this divine centre. We are challenged to embody the Christ energy.

How then? What does it mean to incarnate the Christ, to imitate the Christ? In *The Way of the Dream*, Marie-Louise von Franz clearly states that we are not called to ape Jesus, but to imitate Christ.[5] We are not called to be "little Jesus's," rather we are summoned to our own *Christification*. Von Franz continues: "Christ, in a way, is the model of a man who went along with his own fate and carried his own cross and fulfilled his own task without wavering or giving in to any collective pressure. That's why we worship him as a man who has become God, as God who becomes man in him. He carries that out."[6] *Christification* implies a process, a way of living. James Hollis in his work, *What Matters Most*, expresses the distinction between Jesus the event in history and the timeless Christ myth by observing that

Jesus is a noun and Christ is a verb.⁷ Christ in human form involves the Christing, the *Christification* of humanity. Virginia Mollenkott explores this process in her work, *Godding*.⁸ The Christ myth is experienced as an embodied process in our unfolding lives.

I have been immersed in the culture of the Christian faith and the stories of Jesus from early childhood. It is not possible for me to separate completely the stories of Jesus and the myth of the Christ. I imagine this will be true of any who has lived in a culture in which the Christian story has been significant. While this is so, the ongoing task is to seek to understand the character of the Christ manifest in Jesus, and to see how this essential character informs my life. It is also the case that our resources are the sacred texts that are brief and more about faith than historical fact. This is coupled with a long Tradition that builds on the faith story. I believe it was Albert Schweitzer who declared many years ago that we couldn't get back to the historical Jesus. In my experience within my Tradition, the Jesus of history and the Christ of myth are intricately interwoven. To bring the myth forward in my life, to search for the deeper character of the Christ in Jesus, requires thoughtful reflection. It is to embody in my living my understanding of the agenda of Jesus.

For me, one helpful resource in addressing this are the global visual arts and the expressions of images based on the Jesus stories. Jesus, expressed in the visual arts of India, China, Kenya, Haiti, Korea, England, Sweden, in aboriginal cultures and countless others, appears in local forms and physical appearances. He has been localised, acculturated, and has little resemblance to a first century young Jewish carpenter man, however he may have looked! It is noteworthy that in many of the depictions of the infant Jesus he is seen as naked. This highlights the notion of the vulnerability of the Christ image mentioned earlier. If we can be flexible about the appearance, we may be able to create an imaginative space in which to reflect on the expression of the Christ archetype in our own 21st century lives. Our times and issues are vastly different.

Our sacred stories are rich and yet limited, and in these we look for the essential character, the agenda of the Christ myth expressed in the historical man Jesus. From my reading of the sacred texts, and influenced by experiences in my faith Tradition, I seek again this year to distil essential qualities of the Christ – archetype, symbol, myth and timeless truth – that the divine energy incarnates, embodies, in this man, qualities that can inform my efforts to internalise and embody the Christ myth in my soul and my daily living.

As I reflect, I do not want to end up with some pastel picture of the "perfect" Jesus. I want something, someone, to whom I can relate fully as companion in our shared agenda, the *Christification* of humanity. I set these reflections here in present tense language to see if it helps me connect more deeply to it, to him, to the Christ energy in Jesus.

At this time in my life the Jesus I see that helps me reflect on the Christ task includes a sense of being utterly grounded in a relationship with divinity, with God. It consumes him, it contains him; this is his centre. He gives it priority in times of silence and solitude; it is an intimate bond, expressed in one instance as "Abba, father." From this deep bond he is defined from within himself and is fully himself, and from this centre he is sensitive to his time and place and deeply involved with others.

This Jesus has only one master; this is his non-negotiable truth. In this instance he is an "either/or" man. I am challenged to commit to the same … one master. There can only be one number one. Jesus expresses a Christ energy that is deeply compassionate; he feels deeply the pain of others. He is determined to encourage others and to make life better where he can. He also gets pissed off, impatient and angry, and he grieves. He is fierce in his care for the oppressed and disenfranchised.

Jesus embodies a Christ who listens; he seems accepting of people where they are, and he asks questions in order to provoke something new. When he teaches it is with sharp clarity. He does not step back from disagreement. He is clear about consequences for our actions; he is not sentimental. He heals by touch and by presence. He suffers for others willingly; it is for him a form of love.

Having set out these characteristics it seems the challenge is not resolved in a list of specific character traits. Jesus fulfils his task, his destiny, himself. My challenge is to fulfil myself, to become who I am meant to be, who I am destined to be, who I am summoned to be. "Become what you are," is the maxim of the Greek poet Pindar.[9] To be summoned recognises that something deeper than my individual consciousness is influencing my life and its expression. I live in a world larger than myself, and this includes the presence of the Christ within. Lived out in our cultures, our times and places, the specific ways that we do this will emerge out of the ongoing dialogue between our individual consciousness and the energy of the Christ myth rising out from our depths. In appearance the showing forth of the Christ energy in me, living the Christ myth, may look nothing like that energy expressed in Jesus of Nazareth, but it will be mine. This will be me being fully myself engaging that deeper, larger life of the Christ within me.

I have designed a poster that reads:

> "There is no greater challenge,
> no more noble calling,
> than to be me, none other,
> simply me, all of me,
> in the midst of us,
> all of us."

On the surface and in the everyday of our lives, our journey into being simply ourselves and none other may look nothing like the story of Jesus in its historical expression but may well resonate deeply with his character and his agenda.

While I realise that I still refer to the historical Jesus in reflecting on the Christ myth, there is a gender issue here for women that reinforces our need to reflect more deeply on the images of the Christ in Jesus and the Christ in us. We, both women and men, need sacred images and stories of the Christ as woman in order to enrich the imagery of the Tradition. This complementary imagery includes not only the woman-Christ who feeds and nurtures, who heals and teaches, but also the woman-Christ who speaks her truth without apology. We need women-Christs who will suffer with those who face discrimination, oppression and violation, and women-Christs who grieve the tragic injustices and failings of humanity. We need women-Christs who rejoice in community, who share deeply in the lives of others, women-Christs who breathe compassion into the lives of others through their very presence. I would think it is a welcome challenge for women to claim this rich heritage and present reality of Christ in woman. It is also a liberating benefit for men as well to see her, the woman-Christ in countless forms and images. Kathleen Fischer in her work, *Women at the Well*, engages this issue extensively in chapter four on 'Jesus and Women.'[10] She takes it further in stating that, "Jesus of Nazareth in a resurrection body transcends all human limitations, including human maleness. The risen Christ becomes One Body with us all."[11] When we embrace the inclusive gender imagery that is very much a part of our present spiritual and social agendas, we enrich the liveliness of the Christ myth that we bring forward. A rich soulscape is here to explore further, one that includes and moves beyond gender.

It is appropriate of course at this time of year to recall the birth narratives in our tradition. The stories of the infant and his parents in the manger, the visits of shepherds and wise men are rich with symbolic energy that will enrich our understanding of Incarnation. To turn from revering the stories of the past to bringing the truth of Incarnation forward requires us to step into the Christ myth in our own times and places. Unless we do, we are left with a museum piece and the myth dies. It is within us, both women and men, in successive generations, that the Christ myth is carried forward as we acknowledge and engage the sacred Christ energy as the container for our outer lives and the anchor for our inner lives. This Christ is the vital inner core and living wisdom of our being from which the *Christification* of our lives unfolds in common with one another.

I have no conclusion here, only more on which to reflect, and by which to be enthused, amazed, and challenged in the Christmas festival.

Endnotes

1. Wolff, Hanna. *Jesus the Therapist.* p. 65.
2. Sanford, John. A. *The Kingdom Within.* p. 51.
3. Jung, Carl. G. *Memories, Dreams, Reflections.* p. 332.

4. Ibid. p. 328.
5. von Franz, Marie-Louise . and Boa, Fraser. *The Way of the Dream.* p. 184.
6. Ibid. p. 186.
7. Hollis, James. *What Matters Most.* p. 108.
8. Mollenkott, Virginia. *Godding.*
9. Geoghegan, William. D. *Jung's Psychology.* p. 15.
10. Fischer, Kathleen. *Women at the Well.* pp. 75ff.
11. Ibid. p. 79.

References

Fischer, Kathleen. 1988/1989. *Women at the Well: Feminist Perspectives on Spiritual Direction.* London: SPCK.

Geoghegan, William. D. 2002. *Jung's Psychology: As A Spiritual Practice & Way of Life.* Lanham: University Press of America.

Hollis, James. 2009. *What Matters Most: Living a More Considered Life.* New York: Gotham Books.

Jung, Carl. G. 1961. Aniela Jaffe, Ed. *Memories, Dreams, Reflections.* New York: Random House.

Mollenkott, Virginia. 1987. *Godding: Human Responsibility and the Bible.* New York: Crossroad.

Sanford, John. A. 1970/1987. *The Kingdom Within: The Inner Meaning of Jesus' Sayings.* New York: HarperSanFrancisco.

von Franz, Marie-Louise. and Boa, Fraser. 1988. *The Way of the Dream.* Toronto: Windrose Films Ltd.

Wolff, Hanna. 1978/1987. *Jesus the Therapist.* Oak Park: Meyer-Stone Books.

What if?
Reconsidering My Shadow

I composed this reflection in mid-year 2022 in response to the experiences I share at the beginning of the essay. I realise some of the ideas here have been gestating in me for years and represent changes in both my thinking and the images I choose to use. While the references to the Shadow are male and my American culture of origin is a central focus, I hope that others will be able to relate to the issues and challenges that I engage.

Three Stories

"The war is over." That's the way the dream began. Actually, it happened twice. The first time was in May 2018, and the second was in February 2022. Both dreams began with this simple declaration: "The war is over." In the first dream, the English and German prisoners of war were making their journeys home to return to their loved ones and lives. In the second dream, plans were being made by the original inhabitants of the land to negotiate with the victorious colonials to now leave the land to make way for complete local independence and self-determination. The war is over. *What if?*

Several months ago, my colleague, Wilhelm Verwoerd, sent me an article entitled, "*Ubuntu* and the Individuation Process: Toward a Multicultural Analytical Psychology," by Roger Brooke.[1] Brooke raises several issues about Jung's early work, especially in reference to his encounter with black peoples in Africa. On reading this article, I have been left wondering again about the racial implications of the common descriptions of our Shadow experiences as dark, black, primitive, feral, inferior, undesirable, shameful, unattractive, dangerous, and even evil. Wilhelm and I also spent some time reflecting on a photograph of a painting. It shows a person hugging the Shadow. We assumed that the person painted black was the Shadow. We considered it a fair assumption, and it led to considerable conversation about how we imagine and depict the Shadow. To depict the Shadow as black has serious implications for people of color, and indeed for all of us. What are the racial implications of seeing the Shadow as dark or black? What is the outcome for people of color, and for race relations, when we imagine and depict the color of Shadow as dark, and add to this some or all the words listed above? At one point Wilhelm asked the artist in me what color *I* would use to represent my Shadow. *What if?*

Shortly after this I found myself in turmoil; several things added together to stir me up, including computer issues and some considerable tension over Covid protocols and interpersonal differences over vaccinations and mask wearing. Feeling a bit chaotic and upset, I created the space to enter an active imagination. My active imagination experiences usually take place in my inner village where I meet the characters of my inner family. In this instance I engaged in conversation with the Christ, the Christ of my experience and understanding. My Christ image is a central figure in my village circle. We spoke briefly and he suggested some specific and practical actions to help resolve some of my tension. He then surprised me with this statement: "Note George, The Shadow seeks to serve you – he is not your enemy! He seeks to help." *What if?*

In my times of quiet reflection, these three experiences keep emerging. I have decided finally to explore the Shadow in reference to these three incidents, though I respond to the inner summons to enter Shadowland with some hesitation. Volumes have been written by many about the Shadow starting with Jung's own work and including my own reflections in previous presentations and writings. I keep wondering what I can possibly add to all that we have available. I intend to take a more personal approach primarily to clarify my ever-changing ideas and understandings. I am motivated to reflect in response to these three experiences and hope to consider insights and ways forward that are useful to me and to others. I hope these personal reflections on my experiences will be a catalyst for others to explore this relationship in the soul. Some of the questions that sit with me are:

How is it possible that the war is over; what can this mean for me?
   In my imagination how do I depict the Shadow?
      How does the Shadow serve me, help me?
         What if?

Engaging the issues

"The war is over." *What if?* I find myself wanting to reframe my understanding of the Shadow. For years, decades really, I imagined unconsciously the relationship with the Shadow to be essentially adversarial in nature. I have used such phrases as the troublesome Other or the mysterious Other. He has been the one who makes my conscious self uncomfortable, embarrassed, ashamed, and even frightened at times. There have been times when my awareness of him in his more violent moments made me wonder how I could hold my complex self together. This divisive approach to the Shadow relationship no longer appeals to me; it just doesn't work. While in a Jungian framework there is significant emphasis on the integration of the Shadow through inner work, it seems to me that it is still a somewhat conflicted and distant relationship. The declaration from the unconscious dream spirit that "The war is over," pushes me to wonder how to see this relationship differently. I want to move from an adversarial relationship with the Shadow to one of companionship. I want to explore the possibility of our opposition being complementary and not conflicted. This is a complementarity that supports wholeness, and I believe reflects Jung's original sense of the relationship or opposite energies in the psyche. I also do not intend to strip the Shadow of his intensity and passion. To attempt to neuter the Shadow, to minimize the tense, complex and different attitudes and opinions often revealed through the Shadow, and that are part of me, would be damaging to my soul. It would be folly.

Regardless of how often I stumble into either/or thinking at times, I aspire to have "both-and" as the fundamental framework here. I continue to aspire to radical inclusivity, to a "both-and" world. If I commit to radical inclusivity, I can't continue the war, or try to ignore Shadow parts of me who are in my story, in the village. Radical inclusivity means simply the Shadow is in – all in. I am prepared to consider that he performs a valuable task for me, and I want to honor this and learn to love him and include him in the village. In 1975 I heard Dr. Margaret Mead speak at a conference on Mystery at Grace Cathedral in San Francisco. In talking about the larger human community, she used the odd phrase, "include no one out." It has stayed with me and is applicable here. Wholeness, radical inclusivity, requires that the Shadow is in – all in. *What if?*

Among my various activities I function as an artist. Most of my work is in paint and collage. Reclaiming my art interest some thirty years ago has been a substantial blessing in terms of my sense of completeness. This creative activity fairly pulses with life. Each time I sit down and get to work, I seem to enter a different place within myself. It is vibrant, numinous and life giving for me. Wilhelm posed the question to this artist in me. What color would I choose to use to depict my Shadow?

So, where do I go with this provocative question? I brooded over this in my reflections. What about a really smart navy blue or dark red – cool and sophisticated colors? I remember that Jung is credited with the observation that the Shadow is something like 90% gold. I have both spoken and written about the golden Shadow, so how about a golden Shadow? Despite the association of gold with the Shadow, this is a radical shift from the usual associated images. Also, it does not address the potential implications for discrimination against people of color that are associated with the image of the Shadow as black.

Then one morning in my journal writing time I found myself suddenly wondering *what if?* What if my Shadow is the same skin tone as me? What if he is about my height, weight, and age? What if he looks like me, what if we look like twins? This was startling and yet made sense. Someone in me said, "Yes, of course."

The tragic outcomes of unconsciously depicting the Shadow as dark or black became more clear than ever for me when I encountered the book *African Americans and Jungian Psychology: Leaving the Shadows,* by Fanny Brewster.[2] It has been an helpful, important and challenging encounter. Reflecting on Brewster's work has brought back a flood of memories of, and insights into, my own experiences of growing up and living in the cultural reality of racism. I have come to understand more clearly how ignorant I was, and am, of the appalling history of slavery and its heritage in my home country, and of the cruelty and evil that has been inflicted on African American people. I was vaguely aware and not aware. The childhood and teenage memories include times of fear and awkwardness, and times of feeling different and insecure. In the schools from grade seven we were mixed in together, but I don't see it as integrated. We lived in two separate and divided worlds in a quietly divided town. While we did attend dances together in my teenaged years, there was no mixing among families in the homes that I recall. My church congregation was white except for one soprano in the choir. There was no clear awareness of the historical burden that African American people carried through the legacy of slavery. I remember no conscious awareness of what Brewster labels as collective white racism.

The memories of my young years are mixed. While composing this reflection, I made a list of positive encounters with African American peers and others from those growing up years, and it is surprising how much I recall. Two memories stand out for me as enduring and formative. At age eight I was kept home from school for a semester with a heart condition. At first, I was mostly confined to bed and home, and had carers come in during the day to be with me while my mother continued to go to work. Such was the nature of a single parent home with no other income. During this time I had two carers. The first was a kind, older white woman who was with me for a very short time. The second was a lovely young African American woman. She was my only daytime companion for what seemed to be a long time. She was very kind to me; she was my friend. I don't now remember what we did, but seventy-two years later I still remember her kindness and my sense of being safe and well cared for.

As a teenaged boy in high school, I landed a part time job in a hospital kitchen doing cleaning chores of various kinds. The kitchen was adjacent to the hospital cafeteria where the staff took our breaks. I remember sitting at a table near a group of African American women, older women, and listening to their conversation. What I remember was the essential wisdom for life that I heard exchanged. It was impressive to me; I admired them and what I heard. I also remember feeling accepted in friendly ways as a kid of value as we went about our various tasks. Along with these memories, both my family and my faith tradition would have encouraged equality and respect, though the social divisions remained pretty much in place.

In my tertiary years my awareness of our cultural history grew considerably, but the sense of discomfort and separation was well entrenched from my childhood. I knew and did not know. In my middle-aged years, during a brief time working at a conference centre in the eastern United States with people of various ethnicities, especially African Americans, I became more aware of the struggles of the present time around the issues generated by slavery, but still did not grasp the depth of suffering Brewster clearly identifies. In an unexpected experience of synchronicity, during the time of composing this present reflection, I read

Geraldine Brook's new novel, *Horse*, that engages the experience of slavery in depth around horse racing in the American pre-Civil War era.[3] The story has given me more insight into the deep emotional suffering of African American people living in that time, and of the burden of that legacy on African American people now.

Two things are true: on the one hand, from my family and faith traditions and personal experiences, I am governed by the strong conscious desire to treat people as equals, including all people of color. On the other hand, I am plagued by the mostly unconscious collective white racism influenced by my culture and our shared history of the place of African Americans in the story as slaves, people who were no people, brutally dehumanized for economic gain. My world view was contaminated by the silence in my childhood, and I am left with an awkward sense of connection. I am limited by my ignorance and a natural ambivalence toward difference. Both are true, an unconscious heritage and a conscious desire, and at times I am suspended between the two. There is tension, ambivalence in me because of my lived experiences and those unconscious cultural influences.

The article by Brooke and the book by Brewster, along with my lived experiences and my strong desire to embody a life of equality of genders and skin colors, together heighten for me the importance of my images of the Shadow. In terms of racial healing, it makes a difference as to what color I imagine and choose to depict the Shadow. In terms of *my* healing, it makes a difference what color I imagine and choose to depict *my* Shadow. I see more clearly than ever how destructive it is to use dark and negative terms for the Shadow image. While my Shadow carries much that my conscious mind sees as negative under the influence of family, faith, and culture, I am challenged to re-imagine psycho-spiritual images of my Shadow that separate me from the long-standing cultural tradition of projecting negatively onto people of color including African Americans. It is an unconscious projection that continues to be dehumanizing and devastating for people of color and that thwarts the wellness of us all.

Individual souls and a collective culture divided negatively on skin color cannot uphold social justice, promote human equality, protect human dignity, support mental health, and sustain nonviolence. Until I commit to an ongoing engagement with my Shadow, I risk perpetuating the divisive Shadow war within my soul and continue to contribute to the fears and negative projections that are tragically present in communities in which white people and people of color live together.

There are two other matters raised that are part of this reflection. Both matters are raised by the Jungian Analyst James Hillman in his work and picked up by Brewster. Hillman makes a distinction between archetypal psychology and political psychology.[4] The invitation is to realise that we use the word "black" differently in different contexts.

It seems to me that it is possible to draw out three distinctions here: black as expressed in archetypal psychology, black as expressed in ethnic and political contexts, and black as experienced in physical nature. Can we make these distinctions concerning the color black? To some degree it seems possible to make the separations consciously. To focus consciously on the use of the term in various ways allows us to realise that our use of the term "black" with negative connotations may be shifted by choice. While black as I experience it in nature, or in my own psychic material, may carry associations of mystery, anxiety, fear, the unknown, the undesirable and even danger, it is not necessary for me to carry these projections over into my engagements with people whose skin color is dark and different from mine. I have written elsewhere about the treasures of darkness in an attempt to re-engage positive associations with darkness to balance those associations that are negative, and fear based. Consciousness enlarges our capacity to choose, enables a certain degree of freedom, and facilitates a greater capacity to engage difference positively. The ways of the unconscious are not so tidy and do not make this a simple matter. The cultural teachings of my youth are deeply entrenched in me, but they can be managed differently and more consciously if I am prepared to address the stirrings of my Shadow as they arise and exercise conscious and thoughtful responses to those persons who are different from me. While Shadow work is ongoing, consciousness does free me to exercise a greater freedom to choose how to be in the world.

The second matter that Hillman raises, and that Brewster includes in her work is an historical note on our use of the words black and white to distinguish between peoples. Hillman asserts that the term "black" was first used to describe African people by English speaking sailors in the 15th century. The term "white" to designate an ethnic group was subsequently used early in the 17th century, and became the term used for Christians by 1680.[5] The moralization of the terms in socio-political contexts would have easily developed through these distinctions of differences. The entire enterprise of the enslavement of African peoples could easily have grown out of this limited understanding of differences as whites took superior status over blacks. If we can understand this consciously, we need not unconsciously be subject to the associations of the past in forming our relationships in the present and for the future. It is not necessary or inevitable for African Americans or any peoples of color to carry the negative Shadow projections of white communities. To develop an awareness of this history and the resultant issues enables us to choose to act for human equality, dignity, and respect.

A new image

The three experiences with which I began, and the subsequent reflections around them, invite me to give serious consideration as to how to reframe my understanding and my language and images of the Shadow. The dreams invite me to consider how the war is over. The question from Wilhelm invites me to ponder visual associations of color with the Shadow, both personal and collective. The statement by the Christ of my imagination invites me to think beyond a conflicted relationship with Shadow. How will I reframe the Shadow experiences? What color will I choose to depict the Shadow? How is it that the war is over? *What if?*

The *what if* questions from the journal writing mentioned earlier seems an appropriate starting place. In terms of color, it makes sense to me to imagine my Shadow as having the same skin tone as me. He looks like me, same age, height, and weight. We do seem like twins. In my imaginal wanderings I have seen him with a great pack on his back. He carries it willingly as it is his job for us. It contains all that I have not wanted to know, or face up to, all that has shamed me, embarrassed me, all that has set me at odds with my People, my culture and faith tradition, all that has differed from my righteous conscious self. His pack holds the past Shadow qualities that have been engaged and claimed and carries the ongoing Shadow qualities as well that continue to emerge in new experiences and new projections. He lugs around on his back all who I have not wanted to be, and who I hesitate to get to know. I asked him once if we could take it off his back and set it down. He indicated that this is his job for us, and he does it willingly. He did suggest that we go through the pack from time to time to see what is now there and what has been added.

Where is he standing, my twin? Right next to me, he goes wherever I go. He very often offers a quite different response to whatever is being considered. He whispers or mutters within me what I would not say aloud. How are we together? I realise that I am coming to love him for who he is and how he serves us in the village. He is a loyal companion and without him, I am half a man. I imagine that photo of the painting with the two persons hugging that Wilhelm and I considered. In mt present imagination we are now the same color, twins hugging, and it is difficult at times to tell us apart. *What if?*

Thinking the Unthinkable

Is this possible? Is it possible that the war can be over? I was stuck here and not sure how to proceed, and then had one of those synchronistic experiences. At the time I was also looking for a novel to re-read, and my hand went to the novel *Ransom*, by David Malouf. I was startled to find in the front of the book in my personal index a notation of a passage that inspired me forward. In the novel King Priam of Troy discusses with Hecuba, his wife, his plan to recover the body of their son Hector from Achilles. She sees his plan as foolish, impossible. He replies: "The fact that it has never been done, that it is novel, unthinkable – except that *I* have thought it – is just what makes me believe it should be attempted. It is possible because it is not possible."[6]

The challenge for me, the invitation, is to make the attempt to stop the conflict with the Shadow, to drop the defensive, battle-ready attitude toward my other, and to embrace the one I thought mistakenly was my enemy. He is different from my ordinary, limited conscious understanding of myself and my views of life. He is a piece of work as we say, and yet a valued family member in the village. Without him, without my Shadow, there is no hope of any appreciable, sustained wholeness. Without making peace with him, the battles and skirmishes will continue endlessly, and he will interfere at times with how I want to be in the world.

Is it unthinkable? Priam considers this in his conversation with Hecuba as he considers his plan. Jung, in his memoir, *Memories, Dreams, Reflections*, speaks of his struggle as a young man with an unthinkable thought. He struggles against it for a time and finally yields to it. With thinking the unthinkable thought came "an indescribable relief" and a sense of grace and bliss. Jung goes on to connect this surrender in the struggle with aligning oneself with the will of God.[7] What may be the Godly challenge, the challenge from our deepest wisdom, is to climb out of our boxes, our comfort zones, and to claim the Shadow we have denied, to think the unthinkable, and to consider possible the not possible. In this instance, to declare that the war is over is to claim my Shadow as my own, my brother, my twin, my companion. For me, it also affirms that I am meant to withdraw as much as possible my unconscious projections on those many "others" in my outer life. The projections may remain, for they provide an energy for living, but if I am conscious of them and acknowledge them internally, they need not be harmful to others.

The benefits of this bond with my twin are for me many and dramatic. I surrender to a more honest, humble self-understanding and self-acceptance. I feel safer and at home with me, more grounded with a down to earth sense of myself living on level ground with others. I will be less susceptible to inflation and unconscious self-righteousness. Yes, I realise that I am much like others. We all are a people who struggle with the complexities and mysteries of being human. This can release in me a greater compassion for others who also struggle to love their Shadow companions. Having claimed the simple reality of my Shadow companion, I am less at the mercy of my unconscious, feral emotions, and surprising outbursts of various angers. I am more able to practice a disciplined containment of my Shadow energies and to redirect the energy that has fueled my projections. So much of what has shaped my Shadow twin and fueled my projections is the threat that can come from the encounter with differences in endless forms, including different people, different ideas, and different convictions. If I can hold steady in the face of differences and the possible impact on my world view, I may be able to shift my response to differences from being threatened to being enriched. In my specific experiences with people of a different skin tone, to withdraw those unconscious collective projections that grew in me as I grew up, is to enlarge my capacity for engaging differences that can enrich me and open me to a larger sense of life. Among all these benefits is the truth that I am more able to contribute a more compassionate, transforming, and redemptive energy to the Common Good. My Shadow work has ongoing and sacred benefits for others.

To withdraw my projections onto countless others, including people of color, to reclaim myself in my fulness as best I am able, and to work toward this deep self-acceptance and self-responsibility, is to bring the war to an end. To learn to love and value the Shadow within my village as my helper and valued companion is to enrich our journey together into a greater wholeness. This unthinkable, yet sensible undertaking is to offer great blessing for the Common Good. To paraphrase Priam, King of Troy in the novel, if it seems impossible it may well be possible, and I am summoned to attempt it. *What if?*

In my journal reflections one morning, my twin and I spoke about an aspect of us that is resistant to change. I asked if we could remove him from the backpack and redirect his energy. He replied and we continued:

	Yes. No. Maybe.
Is this finished?	*No.*
Will it ever be?	*No.*
Can we be companions?	*We already are.*
This doesn't feel tidy.	*It isn't.*
Do I need to fear you?	*Only if you ignore me.*
Life's not simple.	*True.*
I'm confused.	*Stand firm!*
Where?	*Here.*

What if?

What if I surrender and admit that you are here ... and I mean right here ... here next to me ... looking at me in silence ...?

What if I realise how much you look like me, same skin color, same height, same weight, same hair color, and you wear glasses too ...?

What if I open my tense and hesitant arms to you, embrace you, and hold you close to my body ...?

What if I admit that you are not my enemy and let our war be over ...?

What if I call you brother as we lay our heads on each other's shoulders and let the tears fall ...?

What if I with you look into the pack on your back and acknowledge all that you carry of me ... of us ...?

What if I thank you for carrying all of me that I have been trained to deny, dismiss, avoid, dislike ...?

What if I realise that I am beginning to love you ... to realise that I need you ... that without you I am incomplete ... half a person at best ...?

What if I realise that without you, I am a danger to myself and to others ...?

What if sometimes we laugh with each other and are pleased with our company ...

What if I let you hold my hand as we stand together and engage the world ... our world ...?

What if ...?

Endnotes

1. Brooke, Roger. *Ubuntu and the Individuation Process:* pp. 36–53.
2. Brewster, Fanny. *African Americans and Jungian Psychology: Leaving the Shadows.*
3. Brooks, Geraldine. *Horse.*
4. Brewster, Op. Cit. p. 110.
5. Brewster, Ibid. p. 112.
6. Malouf, David. *Ransom.* p. 59.
7. Jung, C. G. *Memories, Dreams Reflections.* pp. 36–40.

References

Brewster, Fanny. 2017. *African Americans and Jungian Psychology: Leaving the Shadows.* London: Routledge.

Brooke, Roger. 2008. *Ubuntu and the Individuation Process: Toward a Multicultural Analytical Psychology.* in *Psychological Perspectives.* 51:1.

DOI: 10. 1080/00332920802031870.

Brooks, Geraldine. 2022. *Horse.* Sydney: Hatchette Australia.

Jung, C. G. 1961. Aniela Jaffe, Ed. *Memories, Dreams Reflections.* New York: Pantheon Books.

Malouf, David. 2009. *Ransom.* Penguin Books Australia.

Afterword

Twelve essays and many years along, I keep coming back to two basic experiences in my own reflections: gratitude and change.

These essays affirm again for me that the psychological work of Carl Jung's psychological work has a great deal to offer the spiritual practices of any religious tradition. I continue to be committed to the integration between the two in my spiritual practices and work.

A review of this collection evokes in me a simple sense of gratitude. These essays here are like the tip of an iceberg in terms of the countless opportunities I have been given to reflect and share with others about spirited practices that matter to me. There have been so many, and I am grateful. In Twelve Step work for recovery from addiction, the phrase "gratitude attitude" describes an essential part of becoming well and sustaining that wellness. Joanna Macy, in her book with Chris Johnstone, *Active Hope*, promotes gratitude as the starting point toward finding one's place in the Work that Reconnects.[1] In their work *All Things Shining*, Hubert Dreyfuss and Sean Dorrance Kelly assert that in the Homeric period of Greek culture gratitude and wonder were the central characteristics of virtue.[2]

For me, gratitude has the potential to remind us that our lives are lived out in a larger frame than our own efforts, talents, and skills. Something deeper, broader, wider, longer, something mysterious and energizing, something timeless moves through us and our creative expressions and binds us together. There's much more to the iceberg than just the tip we see, or in this case, compose.

I am grateful to the countless people in various places through these decades who have contributed to my life and insights. The lives and stories of many are woven into the fabric of my life and have contributed to the creation of the stories and insights shared here in these essays. Each presentation reworked here into this collection, and each reflection created for this anthology of ideas, represents a privilege for which I am grateful.

I come to the end of this exercise feeling somewhat bemused. In reviewing the twelve essays I realise that my points of view are not consistent over time. We change, times and cultures change, language changes, and I continue to change. In this collection I have put a date on each of these offerings. The original forms of these essays were created in specific times and places and for specific people. In spite of how I have shifted my perspectives over time, I hope that each essay contains something that continues to be useful for others. On one level of life, it seems true that change is constant, and we are forever a People between visions. On another I affirm that our changing lives rest on a deep unchanging bedrock foundation of principles that serve to anchor us in our mysterious life journeys.

Gratitude and change have the potential to fuel hope. What has gone well in the past can act as a foundation for hope as we look forward. It is so for me. The work here and the responses to it over the years have continued to energise my hope for our shared life, the Common Good. I have seen lives transform and ignite with strength and new courage as people have undertaken their soul work. This soul work has included listening to the dreams, using their wounds and failings as great teachers for the shaping of life, accepting what cannot be changed and changing what can be changed, coping with the ultimate mystery of life, and continuing to explore for meaning and purpose in this awesome life adventure. It has involved creating spiritual practices around personal experiences and making use of the tools of whatever rituals and images from various faith traditions are still of value. All this vibrant, vital change and transformation can increase our capacity for compassion for others and therefore contributes to the Common Good, our life together as we move forward – and this is the only life-giving direction in which we can, in fact, move. Gratitude, change and hope … forward.

Endnotes

1. Macy, Joanna and Johnstone, Chris. *Active Hope*. p. 6.
2. Dreyfus, Hubert and Kelly, Sean Dorrance. *All Things Shining*. p. 74.

References

Dreyfus, Hubert and Kelly, Sean Dorrance. 2011. *All Things Shining: Reading the Western Classics to Find Meaning in a Secular Age*. New York: Free Press. p. 74.

Macy, Joanna and Johnstone, Chris. 2012. *Active Hope*. Sydney: Finch Press. p. 6.

Acknowledgements

First, I am deeply grateful to those individuals who provided me with opportunities to offer my reflections in a variety of settings. These include retreats, lectures, workshops, and worship events. I am grateful to those who have read all or part of this collection of essays and offered feedback and encouragement. My heartfelt thanks to Victoria Castiglione for reading and offering editorial advice in several key places. Her work has greatly improved the essays, encouraged me, and contributed to my ongoing learning about writing. Thanks as well to Gary Commins who also read and offered notes on the entire collection. Other readers include Norma Dody, Brittain Garrett, Antonia Clissa, Maree White, Matt Lord, Dom Fay, Ashley Brown, Lachlan Savill, Mary Martin Stump, Sally Kester and Gabrielle Dean. I have been well supported in creating this collection, and am grateful.

My thanks to the staff of Independent Ink once again for their quality work in taking my manuscript and producing a book. Ann Wilson, Michelle Van Dyk and Julian Mole have been a pleasure to work with and have enabled me to fulfill my intention to be part of the larger conversations that explore how to cultivate peace and embrace the challenges of nonviolent living.

Contributing to the conversations for peace ...

www.ingramcontent.com/pod-product-compliance
Lightning Source LLC
Chambersburg PA
CBHW050309010526
44107CB00055B/2166